THE THREE HOLY KINGS.

An Historical Drama in Five Acts.

BY

FREDERIC EBERSWEILER

OF THE

SOCIETY OF JESUS.

Translated from the German
by a Member of the same Society.

O wondrous Mother of the Saviour
Be thine this work of ours.

Second, Revised Edition.

St. Louis, Mo. 1906.
Published by B. HERDER,
17 South Broadway.

COPYRIGHT BY

JOSEPH GUMMERSBACH.

1904.

—BECKTOLD—
PRINTING AND BOOK MFG. CO.
ST. LOUIS, MO.

PREFACE.

"The Three Holy Kings", being an historical drama, is not exclusively a Christmas drama, but may be exhibited at any time of the year.

The subject is the Epiphany of our Lord, — the manifestation of the Word made flesh, evidenced by wonderful events and the fulfilment of prophecies, — the appearance of the Light which enlighteneth every man that cometh into this world, — the coming of Jesus Christ who brings 'peace to men of good will', who rejects the Jews and elects the Gentiles. "He came unto His own and His own received Him not: but as many as received Him, He gave them power to be made the sons of God."

St. Matthew's brief recital of the adoration of the Magi leaves a wide margin to draw from and shape such poetical fictions as give form and expression to what stirred the hearts of men about the period our God became man. Choruses also dwell in lyrical effusions on the lofty ideas which are awakened by the movement of the dramatic plot.

Our narrative agrees with the opinion of those interpreters who, according to a rule of exegesis eschewing the miraculous when not expressly called for, claim that the Star appeared to the Magi in their own country and did not proceed before them on their way to Judea. The Wise Men say in Jerusalem: "We saw His Star *in the East*", that is, in our country, East of Judea.

The dramatic action begins on the Epiphany of the Lord, twelve days after His birth. We allow a lunar month for the journey and finish the action on the fortieth day after the Nativity of Christ, which is the day of His Presentation. St. Luke notes that 'the parents of Jesus carried Him to Jerusalem, to present Him to the Lord', and then 'returned to Nazareth.' The adoration of the Wise Men and the Flight into Egypt must in all probability be admitted as an *intermezzo* on the evening of that self-same day, when the Holy Family, back in Bethlehem, were preparing for their trip home. For the advent of the Kings did not take place after the time of the Presentation, because they found Jesus in Bethlehem not in Nazareth, nor did it take place before that time, because after the departure of the Kings, the Holy Infant could no longer be safely brought to Jerusalem, but had to be rescued by immediate flight from the danger of being murdered with the children of Bethlehem.

The truths which Theology proposes in a scholastic style to the intellect, Catholic poetry offers in their fascinating ideal beauty to the whole soul. If the mere reading of our humble effort enrich any one's mind with a greater knowledge and love of Jesus and delight in the contemplation of His Infinite Beauty, we have gained the reward we coveted.

TRANSLATOR'S NOTE.

The author of this noble drama is a missionary in the Rockies, where he lives a solitary life, laboring for the salvation of the Whites and Indians and applying his few leisure moments to study and composition. Several of his productions have met with praise from the critics of the "Stimmen aus Maria-Laach". Therefore we could wish that our effort were more worthy of them, but we permit it to the kind indulgence of the Catholic public.

THE TRANSLATOR.

THE THREE HOLY KINGS.

Persons Represented.

BALTASSAR, in the vigor of manhood, King of the wealthy Arabians.

CASPAR, a youth, King of Saba and the Isles of the Red Sea.

MELCHIOR, old but robust, King of Tharsis, the Coasts and Isles of the Persian Gulf.

Each of the Three Kings has three Companions.

HEROD, the Tyrant, King of Judea.

CYRINUS, a Roman, Confidant of Herod.

ROMANUS, a Roman, of the Court of Augustus.

OPHNI, High priest.

THE HOLY SIMEON.

BALAC, Brother to Baltassar.

LUCIFER.

MARY with the CHILD JESUS.

ST. JOSEPH.

ANGELS.

A Toll-Collector; SADUC, a Sadducee; PHARES, a Demagogue; ZARAM, a Citizen of Jerusalem; LEVI, a Priest of Bethlehem; two Shepherds; Scribes; the Multitude.

ACT I.

SCENE I. — ARABIA. Throne-room in Baltassar's palace. Baltassar on his throne.

[Enter three Nobles in traveller's attire.]

I Noble. Sire, Ruler of this wealthy Arab land
Behold us here, equipped to grace
A wonder-journey in your company.

Balt. Ah! sooth the worthiest, truest of the realm!
We will straightway upon our desert craft,
Hie to the marvelous Babe with seemly haste.

SCENE II. The Same.

[Enter in haste Balac, casts himself at Baltassar's feet.]

Balac. O Baltassar, I beg, plead — voice and knees!
Forego the fond emprise, to which an ill
Sprite urgeth you today.

Balt.   Our brother, fie!
Calm thy soul's tempest, and with us in peace
Rehearse the miracle that hath bechanced.
Twelve nights ago from out the tower we spied
The starry paths. A faint, faint glimmering
Like to the sparkle of the eye, anon
Peered through the heavens' vault; significant
The orbs looked laughing down, as they'd narrate

To those who dwelt below, that God had life
In store — that soon the mercy-smitten sky
Should bend to earth and drop a priceless jewel!
The universe's dome had shone ne'er so,
Shedding effulgence mid the holy shades.
Yet lo! while they do deepen, suddenly
Looms up anear, the Almighty's very beam
Enlisted 'neath the whirling of the spheres
To be a token in our Orient.
How pure the brilliant, silvery mass of white
Viewed from our lofty capitol, doth shine —
A lordly sun at his high noon — its sweep
Directed towards the home of Jacob's race.
The Prophet's word that so it was to be,
Sends gladness coursing through our veins in
 thrills,
A levin-flash illumes our mind, and clear
The message peals: "He shall be Juda's King—
The Virgin hath conceived and borne a Son!"
Then thankful jubilee wells from our heart,

[*Lifts his hand; swears anew.*]

We register a vow to seek the One
Made mortal for man's sake and offer Him
Our gifts of myrrh, our plighted loyalty.
Meanwhile the lustre wakes the astonished folk
From slumber, and they gather numerous
And stare and ply the question anxiously:
"Whe'er bodes it our felicity or woe?"
We join them and proclaim aloud: "All hail!
Our people, let not fear distress you now:

It is the Saviour's harbinger, foretold
By Balaam two thousand years ago:
The sages long abide what ye have seen;
It freighted comes with tidings of great joy, —
Redemption is at hand for the Elect,
And ere the dawn shall light upon our world."

Thus spake we — only three did comprehend

[*Points to his escort.*]

Our speech: the rest were thunderstruck at it,
And eyed us and the prodigy by turns —
Which clomb and clomb and vanished in the blue.

Balac. Enow of portent-prying foolishness!
Take common sense for guide; it is the safest, sure.

Balt. Ah! Common sense chained to idolatry,
A victim of the dark, mendacious fiend,
Lurketh owl-wise among the nether glooms,
Lest that mayhap which purpling gilds the face
Of things do hurt its fixed and stupid glare.
Bow ye before the sun and moon and stars,
And care not Him who first set them to move?
Ay, gape as tourists, all oblivious,
How came it into being, why despatched,
Though explanation is most patent here.

Balac. You then place confidence in oracles.

Balt. Nay, treat not slightly what the Hebrew scrolls
And our own warranted traditions guard
So jealously of future boons to us:
Through fifty generations scarce a one
Of royal ancestors did not revere.

Balac. Would you then, magic is a wanton art?
    He was an adept in it, whom you laud.

Balt. Who made the she-ass babble prophecy,
    Can force e'en Satan's utterance, so that
    It be infallible. But what doth say
    The genuine recital of our sires?

    As o'er the sandy wastes, a progeny
    From Egypt freed, were nearing our estates,
    The king, a Balac, — brother, thy namesake, —
    Strove subtlely to blast their vaunted might,
    And sent the region's noblest, laden rich
    With gifts, betimes to Chaldee's far renowned
    Soothsayer, Balaam, to have him work
    That ruin. Howbeit e'en his sumpter-beast
    Chid him, recalling what the Vision uttered:
    "My blessing is upon them; curse them not!"
    Still he adown the mountain's rugged brow
    Surveyed th' encampment: — seven altars stood
    About, for worship of the planets reared: —
    And loosed his tongue obedient to behest,
    But benedictions issued forth inspired:
    "A star shall rise from Jacob, and a rod
    Branch out from Israel: He that shall rule
    From Jacob comes, a manful conqueror!"
    And it has risen! My gaze thou'rt favored —Ay!
    Greeted by the new-born Deliverer's sign,
    As He descends to break sin's galling yoke,
    Soon to display His own sweet countenance.

II Noble. And Balaam in his sons sees Him — in us,
    The star-experienced Magi.

THE THREE KINGS.

All three Nobles.   We must to Him!

Balac. Ah blind infatuation! Certes ye've
    Read on its disk: "The Star of Balaam!"

Balt. So told its sheen and course: for be assured,
    To Him no word is yet impossible.

Balac. The infant finds amazement everywhere.

Balt. The zany does not find it anywhere.
    A special grace upon our soul this hour
    Has wrought in flames of loves: "The Star of
        Christ!"
    The meaning not ambiguous conveyed.
    So bides our resolution firm as flint:
    Who did aught great that nothing dares to risk?

                [To his escort.]

    Let's off! We'll risk our all in wistful search
    For Him who for us men is man become.

Balac. And after vain illusion's proved a dream,
    We shall salute you royal simpleton.

Balt. And after faithful trust has given us fame,
    Ye shall salute us royal Wisdom's son.

        SCENE III.   The Same.
           [Clamors outside.]

    Long live the Lord of Saba and the Isles!

III Noble Balt. As I have sight, 'tis Erythrea's liege,
    The sovereign of the main and skirting coasts,
    Your youthful friend, your cherished brother-king,
    Gaspar!

[Enter Gaspar and escort.]

Gaspar. Hail, Baltassar!

[Falls on Baltassar's neck.]

Balt. Our Gaspar, hail!

Gaspar. Your glance doth query anxiously, O friend,
What might bring us so unexpected here.
Ah! Ruler of this wealthy Arab-land,
We're come to share with you a happiness
Full great: it has been shown to us — the Star
Of happiness.

Balt. Ay? Did you also see...?

Gaspar. We saw enraptured the saving ray:

[Pointing to his Companions.]

And these, the very columns, of our state,
Enjoyed with us the selfsame privilege.

Balt. A heart's deepfelt congratulations.

[Embracing him.]

And these,
Our kingdom's pride, have also been the blessed
Associates in a similar benefit.

[Points to them.]

All three Nobles Gasp. Praised be the bounty that to subject thus

And ruler hath shown forth a father's care!

Balt. We thank Thee on Thy gift sublime, O Sire
Illuminate for aye! — Thou sacred Night!

Thou God-loved Night! In whose own middle course
He that with unapproached splendor dwells,
Concealed His lustre 'neath a human shape,
And sent, auspicious to heathendom,
His Star that it might beckon us to Him.

Gaspar. When saw you it?

Balt. From our observance at Midnight.

Gaspar. We in the rising blush of morn,
Twelve days ago, when—'tis our wont—we made
Thankful the sacrifice fume, incense-sweet,
To Him who with each day reneweth life,
The Author of our being — and our all, —
Beheld displayed a luminary's torch,
Before whose flame e'en Lucifer was dimmed, —
Just where the gray was dappled with the red.
We shuddered, but conviction that the dawn
Of our salvation was then ushered in,
Streamed on our soul brightly, and both our doubt
And wav'ring hesitancy disappeared.
Till sunrise it did shimmer joyfulness,
And fondle from its height our every sense
Enchantingly and bid: "Haste off and seek
The Sun of God which from this day shall glad
The day of man's salvation, prostrate burn
The odors to the Light of light." Forthwith
We order out the dromedaries for
A journey to yourself and then with you
We'll to the land of the Messiah's birth.

Balac. And do your hoary council naught dissuade?

Gaspar. The news raged through our city like a storm,
Gathering our relatives and bride, late wed,
And parents, who upon their knees implored,
The while tears bathed our cheeks: "Avaunt with such
Ill-omened wandering — a fool's resolve!
The people style you now infatuate!"
We told those dear ones that a sapience
Supern had wrought it in our intellect,
Praying the father from whose feeble grasp
We had but lately ta'en the commonwealth,
To ply again its rule till our return.

Balac. A gale right furious is threatening,
And have you left the state to crippled age?

Gaspar. Though it do cost our throne we must and will
See Him! A purpose holily conceived
Is free from all disaster. And thus far
Has fortune favored: she shall favor aye.

SCENE IV. The Same.

[*Flourish of trumpets and shouts.*]

Long live the King of Tharsis.

III Noble Gasp.   Lo! there comes
The hoary Monarch of the Persian Gulf,
Who long hath swayed its tropic wave and shore!

Melch. Hail, Baltassar!

Balt.   Hail, Melchior!

Melch. (*to Gaspar.*) You here!
  Then you are welcome here, our youthful King!
  (*to All.*) Your features blank betray profound surprise.
  The Saviour's Star now hath already shone.

Balt. You too . . .

Gasp. We saw it: therefore 'tis you see Us here.

Balt. And unto each are added three.

Melch. Though He's but one calls us to the God-Man.

All three Nobles Balt. The Father, —

All three Nobles Gasp. and His Wisdom, —

All three Nobles Melch. and His Love.

Gasp. (*to Melch.*) When saw you first its gleam?

Melch. The regal sun's
  Twelve times emerged from out the mere, since we
  At the third hour, the palace left, sat in
  The seat of Justice, justice to dispense
  Unto the throng assembled at the gates, —
  Who greeted us with cheers and pointed where
  The Eastern sky already cast about
  A spell — resplendent in such wondrous wise
  That we were fixed, and moved nor sense nor limb.
  "It is the saving Star!" Ten thousand pealed,
  "At last are expectations realized
  In fact! O sire, despatch an embassy
  And gold in tribute to the Saviour."
  "Ourself," we answer, "forthwith do depart
  With all a king's state to adore our King."

This company we then selected — three,
Exceeding loved each by his well-ruled folk.

Balac. Stupidity I wot is then let loose!

Melch. Not thus it was when in our youth the crown
Became our heritage: with labor could
We hardly banish base idolatry
And rouse the embers of a wholesome hope.
What was so early brave essayed, and brave
Accomplished through maturer years, that now
In meagre pittance is restored, when age
Hath trained its silvered circles on our head.

Balac. Wisdom becometh years: that you attempt
Examine well!

Melch. Examine well? Apace
The peoples' misery and longing moved!
Looked they not towards the chosen Israel
Awaiting the announcement that He's come
Who is to come? They did, and while they looked,
Behold the wondrous Star! We must salute
The Star of Balaam and follow it.
Ay, thou art welcome, heavenly message! Thou
Proclaimest that today which Adam's sons
Four thousand years expect—the Woman's Seed,
To crush the cunning serpent's guile despatched
Beneath His tread. O blessed Star thou know'st
The blessing of our kind! What fortune's ours!
If death appear to blast a waning sight,
E'en death is shorn of terrors by thy ray.

Balac. Old man, the travel is beyond your powers:
It lies through Araby's peninsula,
Then through the sands of the drear desert waste
In which great Moses wandered forty years,
The grave of victims of the Bedouins,
Who prowl unceasingly in quest of spoil.

Melch. (*to All*). Let us display the fortitude begot
Of piety and offer up our life,
If such God's will, in generous sacrifice.

Balt. (*to I Noble*). Go put the caravan in ready trim.

[*Exit I Noble.*]

Balac. 'Tis prudent sooth; ye have bethought the bourne.

Balt. We make for Palestine: thence the Star came.

Gaspar. The city certainly Jerusalem.

Melch. Where ought one seek the royal heir, if not
In the metropolis? Albeit we
Will never rest, until we find Him, though
We journey to the farthest mount of Dan.

Balac. By those who tend the kingdom's merchandise
With creeping horror I have heard described
The proud exclusiveness that marks the Jew,
And Herod's cruel deeds.

Balt.   Nay, brother, cease
To dwell on possible contingencies, —
Suffice thee that such is God's will.

All.   Ay — 'tis
God's will! We're off, off to Jerusalem!

SCENE V. The Same.

[*Double call to march. Reenter I Noble.*]

I Noble Balt. Hear ye the bugle-blast: it summons you.

Balac. Aggrieved I bid you then a long farewell!
　　　　Your hero-mould recks naught of reign or life
　　　　To gain renown: with loftier intent
　　　　Upon these carriers of the wilderness
　　　　Essay you an unheard of expedition.
　　　　Oh may your guide not be the luring light.

Balt. Apply to our affairs, while we're away.

Balac. What bitter tears a faithful spouse shall shed!
　　　　E'en now within your palace' secret dome,
　　　　She is retired afflicted — with your child.

Balt. God'll favor her: be thou her guardian.

[*Embraces him: both weep. Exit Balac.*]

SCENE VI. The Same.

Melch. Let us adore Him, who, so good, so kind, —
　　　　From millions deigned our lowliness to choose.

Strophe I.

Balt. On great Creation's morn the fiat issued from
　　　　　　the Lord
　　　　And through the wide-expanded firmament the
　　　　　　planets adored;
　　　　　　　　Into its round
　　　　　　　　They all poured
　　　　Ay, out of Chaos they did bound

And despatch, prepense,
The glowing, twinkling
Beams that to the enkindled eye revealed
A well-embattled array:
And since they've ever been sprinkling
Or mid the darkness of sombre night
Or mid the gladness of day
The Immortal's unapproachable ray;
But oh! the deep trance filled our every sense
As on Redemption's morn shone forth the radiance,
Participate of the Splendor concealed,
A light from His Light.

ANTISTROPHE I.

All three Nobles Balt.

When God His torches insphered
Them by their names He assembled to trace out their course;
And each of them reared
With thanks to their source
In palpitant jubilation:
How glad this universal structure to order itself with the swiftness of levin
In the far-reaching, intricate choirs
Before the Ruler of Heaven!
"The Lord, He hath called us to show us our station, —
The angel-guide that kindly is given:
Oh haste we, comrades, to blaze all our fires!"

Strophe II.

Melch. Three, Noah's children, issued from the ark,
        When giant generations
        The Deluge had swallowed; —
Our ancestors of new degree,
From them our three continents loom:
        Three simple monarchs we,
Selected from myriad nations,
        Firstling vocations!
Who henceforth numbers uncounted from East
        and from West shall mark,
        Tending, all-hallowed,
        Out of heathendom?
Who mark the homage-bearing Rulers' orations,
        E'en to the last-throned, followed
        By the great doom,
When tumbling from elevate orbits, their stations,
The blood-colored moon and the sun, direful, dark,
        Call those who their light ever viewed
        To the Judge and the Rood!

Antistrophe II.

All three Nobles Melch.
        The God-appointed people's sire
        Hied with the others
        Into the Nile-watered regions; —
And prostrated them before Joseph, the brothers
And he, — the Sun, Moon, eleven Stars were bowed
Before the Saviour of the world!

THE THREE KINGS.

But left not with Moses an army unfurled
    In twelve branches, twelve numerous legions ?
Heeding the guidance by night of the pillar of fire,—
    Traversed the Red Sea's bed with sure-footed pace,—
    They wandered on o'er Arabia's desert face,
        Under the manna-rich cloud,
        To the land of their biding,
          Which God was providing
      For hopefullest Abraham's race.
So visit we twelve the Saviour of men, obeying His
          grace,
    And follow the lustre of His wondrous Star
      E'en to the land of His biding.
      But whoso the star-beams will count,
Counts the Messiah's unceasing adorers who emulate us
    Sprung from the Twelve that no perils daunt
      Sent by the Lord afar
        Unto each place
Beneath the celestial courses circuitous.

Strophe III.

Gasp. Who knows not Saba's Queen, our fair ancestress,
    That to the city of David boldly journeyed on,
A Wisdom unearthly to relish and priceless gifts to
        offer to Solomon?
    With rich-laden camels through deserts we'll press
Forward, a wisdom to gather from Wisdom's self,
      God's only Son.

Antistrophe III.

III Nobles Gasp. When to us the Christ's eyes lift, —
Oh happy! oh happy! we'll cast us down, conscious
to adore,
And hand Him our costliest gift;

[*Gaspar holds aloft a box containing frankincense.*]

Gasp. And welcome shall odorous incense be whiffed,
Awhirl, to God;

[*Balt. points out a casket of myrrh near by.*]

Balt. Welcome too the myrrh from the resinous core
Shall honor man:

[*Melch. shows a box of gold.*]

Melch. The God-Man,
With gold we can
Rejoice Him; He claims forever a world's scepter
rod!

All. Let's off, the Star proceeds! Our Saviour calls!

[*All march out to music. The curtain falls.*]

ACT II.

SCENE I. — JERUSALEM. The City Gate. Sunrise.

[*A Toll-collector on the lookout.*]

Toll-Coll. Volumes of dust ascend, as by a storm
  Uplifted. — Who comes here?
[*Rises.*]
  A caravan!
Ay, Arabs they! All Saba's 'rived! The pass
Is with their dromedaries stol'n from view.
And gems and gold reflect the morning's smile.
What! Diadems the leaders show! They're kings!
They have an escort—white and black and brown!
[*Waits.*]

No doubt the halt will be afore the inn.
Dismounting now — the baggage left untouched.
The kings haste on with nine associates.
How shall Jerusalem marvel at the troop!
[*Ponders.*]

Herod must be informed. Oft to his ear
I've borne news true or false and thus increased
The shekels few that from the public fund
Doth reach our coffers ever and anon.

SCENE II. The Same.

[Enter Melchior.]

Melch. Thanks to the Lord! Success upon our search!
  Hail thou, Jerusalem, thou royal seat!
  Thou rich with towers! Securely thou dost hold
  The world's Salvation in thy festal walls.

[Enter Gaspar and escort.]

Gasp. Thou Sion's mount, thou fane of Solomon,
  Thou joy-engirt! Built on the holy hills,
  Thou city of the Son of God, hail! hail!

[Enter Baltassar.]

Balt. Shine brightly, for thou saw'st the Lamp of Day
  Rise over thee and dart His beams abroad!
  And we have hied, we Kings, unto thy Light.

I Noble Balt. No feast 's kept here! No! The Messiah's place
  Greeteth His advent not with jubilee.

[Looks into the street.]

II Noble Balt. There lists along a self-encompassed prude.

SCENE III. The Same.

[Enter Saduc richly clad. Stops and gapes.]

Balt. O citizen of this the luckiest state,
  Where can the new-born heir be found, the Prince?
  We saw his Star e'en from the Orient,
  And have set out to pay respects to Him.

Saduc [*amazed*] How! What! The new-born Prince, the heir!

No man wots aught of such an one — or His.

Melch. No man? Unfeeling thou! We strangers are,
Yet from the ends of earth His sign obeyed,
While ye, His own, know not your native King.

Balt. Throughout the squares will we proclaim aloud:
O Israel, your King — your King is born!
Attend and let great Sion rouse herself.

Saduc. Tut, tut! there's not a single person here,
For whom I would so rack my precious frame.

II Noble Balt. Thou serpent-tongued!

Gasp. But Juda'll hail in joy
Him now for whom she has long ages looked.

Saduc. A fancy has possessed the vulgar mind,
That soon He walks this race among; and I
Dread much lest a reformer do appear
To nip our pleasures in the laden bud.

III Noble Balt. Speaketh a burgher of the Holy City?

Saduc. As I, so all the rich, who place their trust
In Saduc's word: "Within this life, our life
Stands circumscribed" — the tenet of the Greek,
Of Epicurus, Wisdom's favored child:
"Catch thy delights — they're fleeting — while
thou mayest".

Melch. Amends indeed are needed for man's sin!

III Noble Balt. The worms would not be aught disturbed until
Sated with offal!

Balt. And wast born in ruth,
O great Messiah, unto us, Thy folk!
To lead us by Thy own example to
Spurn fleeting joy? Ah! we will harken — will
Adore: Thy Star's a mighty love produced.

Saduc. What Star? He prates as do the Pharisees
On their traditions oft before the mob.

Balt. The Lord who rules creation sent before
His Star — our angel to conduct us here
Unerringly.

Saduc. Your angels are a myth.
God's no concern in what concerns this earth:
Pretend ye that He's shapen out a star
T' accompany your wandering's every turn.
Weigh well your speech, lest ye become a mock,
Insensate!

III Noble Balt. [*drawing sword*]
Traitor! I will have his life.

Saduc. Mercy! [*Flees. Exit.*]

Balt. Relent:
He's not our subject — nay!

Melch. He's well escaped.

Gasp. May God forgive his taunts!

Balt. Besotted fool, the bounds of his small soul
Hold not the Boundless who with mystery
And marvel dwells engirt — his heart, how black!
Loves lust, not Heaven's will, and therefore in
The shipwreck he hurls safety from his grasp.

THE THREE KINGS.

SCENE IV. The Same.

I Noble Balt. Lo! there comes one in very strange attire.

II Noble Balt. Oh that he may a better welcome give!

[*Enter Phares alone in sack-cloth and ashes,
also Zaram who listens from afar.*]

Balt. Greetings to the Messiah's fellow-townsman!
Where is your Juda's new-born King, prithee?
We've seen His Star e'en in our Eastern land,
And hither we have come, Him to adore.

Phares [*beside himself*] Ye saw then Jacob's Star! And so at last
He hastes to free His Sion! Sion, ah!
Rejoice and cast thy penance-robe aside!
No more thy sons with shaven head shall walk,
By anguish wrung, within thy precincts rare.

[*Pulls off robe.*]

My heart brimful, I dwelt upon thy plaints:
"The time is past, and yet He's not appeared,
Though God did sanction the whole prophecy:
Alas, no safety more for Israel!"
Therefore did I put on the sack, bestrewn
With ashes. [*Casts robe away.*]
Now let jubilee resound.

II Noble Balt. Oh precious hope, He is expected then.

Balt. Where is the town where blessedly He bides?

Phares [*surprised*] How do I know? ye are the very first
To spread these joyful tidings of great joy.

SCENE V. The Same.

Balt. [*approaches Zaram*] Pray, citizen, pray tell where we might seek
    The Prince new-born, the heir of Juda's throne.

Zaram. The Prince new-born? Never expect our Christ
    To view in infant guise. The Son of God —
    His generation who shall e'er relate?
    'Tis the belief, His birthplace shall remain
    Concealed from men.

II Noble Balt.   And so our long, long search
    Is vain.

Balt.   Despair not, for our God's with us.
    [*To Zaram*] But Juda's King remains not e'er concealed?

Zaram. Well, first as man, when He hath spent His youth
    Within the narrow circuit of a village,
    At Jordan's wave He shall display His power,
    Working a miracle for Galilee.
    Then the great Light unto our world appears.
    He comes, a marvel, and selects supreme
    His guard from out of Israel's Twelve Tribes:
    With these He shall besiege Rome and all lands,
    And found a universal empire. Then
    Sion shall give the law to nations — link
    At once of right and love.

Melch.   We too look for
    A cleansing from all sin and a complete
    Deliverance in the Messiah's reign,
    But not the domination of the Jew.

Zaram. Then to Jerusalem, th' earth's metropolis,
　　The treasures of the earth shall streaming flow.

II Noble Balt. Is not this fellow drunk with avarice?

Gasp. We hope for heavenly treasures, stores of grace,
　　Beside these all the gold of earth is dross.

Balt. And were the Saviour poor and full of grief,
　　As Job was, one of our progenitors,
　　We would seek Him e'en in His poverty,
　　Our precious gem, our good, our heritage.

Zaram [*quite angrily*] Then shall no Jew acknowledge Him.
　　　　　　　　　　　　　　[*Turns on his heel. Exit.*]

All.　　　　　　　　　　　　　　　　　Woe! woe!

SCENE VI. The Same.

[*Phares is about to depart*].

Balt. [*to him*] Where lies the palace of King Herod, then?

Phares. Would you essay to find Him at the court?
　　There's no brood there but of the tiger, cubs
　　And tyrants born, not Who, it is foretold,
　　Springs from the lineage of David's house.

Balt. No Idumean's son do we e'er seek.
　　The folk know not the Saviour's abode;
　　A ruler sees much that from them is hidden,
　　And he can gain an entrance to every place.

Phares. I do advise, go not to him.

All [*astonished*]　　　　　　Why not?

Phares. Herod is the Messiah's mortal foe;
　　He hates His followers. And thus you shall

But compromise yourselves and us, if you
Dare question him.

II Noble Balt.   Thou'rt mad.

Phares.   You'll bitter rue
The blind step you propose. Ye are forsooth
The merest strangers in Jerusalem, —
So hear my counsel and then judge withal
Whether my fear is an insanity.

Melch. The wise man probes the consequences of
His deed beforehand; speak thou boldly out.
[*To the rest*] Brethren, we'll list a space.

Phares.   The Prophet's word
Sanctions the common expectation and
The tyrant's dread. Who does not feel, foresee,
What's heavy on the spirits of us all?
Though 'tis a boon to hear that Jacob's word
Outshineth far the many stars and is
Today accomplished anent our eyes.

Balt. Speak; for predictions are a gladsome rede.

Phares. When Jacob from his bed of death, replete
With inspiration, bared unto his sons
Their future destiny, on Juda he
This benediction laid: "The scepter ne'er,
O Juda, shall depart from thee, nor shall
Thy line cease rulers to afford, until
Appears Shiloh, the nations' joy and hope."

SCENE VII. The same.

[*Enter an excited multitude*].

All. Here be they who the great Messiah seek.

Balt. [*aloud*] O citizens, can you make answer, where
    He bides, the new-born King, your Juda's King,
    We saw His Star e'en from the Orient,
    And have set out to pay respects to Him.

All. We know not where.

A Voice.   Be still! the orator!

Phares [*mounting a stone*] Thee, Juda, tribe of kings now
      do I laud!
  When Israel before the Pharaoh fled
  Thou in the van didst walk atween the walls
  Of water through the cleaved surging sea, —
  Thou in the van didst cross the desert, when
  The pillared cloud guided the wandering host,—
  Thou in the van didst enter behind the ark
  O'er Jordan's bed, — didst slay, thy conquering
      hand
  Upon their necks, more Chanaanites than all
  The rest, how faithful to the dictates of God!
  And they bowed down before thee, as thy David
  Mounted the throne with a God-given might.
  Went he to war, who then withstood the Lion
  Of Juda? Laden with spoils he came back:
  Slept he, the Lion, — who dared, who dared to
      wake
  Him from his sleep? His scepter fell betimes
  To Solomon the Wise, richest of rulers,

Under whose sway the land bloomed cheerily,
A vineyard of the choicest, noblest vines.
Then sprouted Jesse's branch five hundred years
Amidst the kings, till withered in the blind
Mathanias. The time of chastisement,
Captivity's long durance, passed away, —
And Babylon fell prostrate. So thy sons
To Sion jubileeing hied, and fought
And built their Temple and their city walls.
A remnant of the others then betook
Them home, freed by the ruin of Ninive.
Thenceforward they conformed their conduct to
The Law, sheltered by the Omnipotent,
Till, an unworthy sprout, vile Antioch,
Would tyrannize, with idols filling all
Thy Temple, all thy streets with flowing blood.
The hero brothers, led by Maccabeus, rose
To win their countless victories on fields
Miraculous! Now a millenium
Is spent and look we for deliverance.
[*Raising his voice.*] For such a royal people never yet
Were destined to endure the galling yoke!
[*Wild and prolonged applause.*]
And in the chains thou gnashing drag'st along
Thou think'st of glories past and hopest still
That they one day shall darkened be by His,
By the Messiah's glory, Light of the world.
[*Wilder applause.*]
Well Herod knew and knows that we but wait
For the Messiah's advent to dethrone
Him.

Some. Come, Deliverer!

All. Messiah, come!

Phares. Therefore long time distrust encompasses
 His troubled soul, and dread, and demons' rage.
 [*To multitude*] Ye citizens of Jerusalem, bethink
 You that these foreigners endeavor to
 Locate Him with King Herod?

[*Confusion and fright.*]

Voices. Do it not!

Others. You will but run us into dangers dire.

Kings and Nobles. How? Why?

Phares. You catch but half how Jacob's Word
 Has been accomplished: list now a moment brief.
 The second half, and then you'll comprehend.
 "Juda, the scepter shall depart from thee!"
 Alas, Rome that subdues the nations round
 Wrested it from the Maccabeans' hand:
 Aristobulus fought against his brother;
 And Pompey, called to aid, took Sion's fort
 Carried Aristobulus off in bonds.
 Thereafter Rome despatched her governors,
 Until Antigonus beneath Antonius' might
 Did fall, murdered — the last of Juda's kings.

[*Shows Roman coin.*]

 We shortly shall relate the overthrow
 Of freedom: thus tells this coin and Cæsar's image.

[*Loud murmurs.*]

 Already Rome, with iron shod, crushes our limbs,
 And places in our David's hallowed seat

The Idumean's cruel, worthless stock.
Herod, a dragon e'er that spitteth fire, —
Thou hast dislodged the Maccabeans — e'en
The last within whose Asmonean veins
Flowed royal blood.

Voices.   Ah, thee to death we grant!

Phares. And thou hast slain our noblest, dragged in chains,
To quench in them the vital spark of freedom, —
While this year we were numbered head by head
Slaves of Augustus. [*Wild murmurs.*] Juda, now, thy scepter
Has gone, — thy tribe has now, now, now ceased long
A legislator to afford. So now
He comes, expected long, who shall be sent.

A Voice. Oh come, beam glad on us, Thou Source of joy!

Phares. Well Herod knows that we expect the advent
Of One to free us from our thraldom — soon.
Anxious, enraged — a bloodhound he awaits Him.
The question fraught with meaning now, you ply:
"Where is the new-born King, great Juda's King?"
You start his fears that there may be revolt
Behind your words — and his suspicion that
They hide conspiracy; enough for him:
As once before, so now he'll massacre
Thousands, anticipating that he dreads.
You bring death to the loved Messiah's friends.

Some Voices. Come not into our city!

All Others. Depart, depart!

Phares. Unless you court the fate of mutineers,
    A direst death! haste ye back to your homes!

Balt. They quail — how timid is the heart of mortals,
    To accomplish what almighty grace designs!
    Trust God! He shall protect you. By Jacob's Word
    You're told that soon there must appear on earth,
    Who shall be the Expected of all men:
    And Jacob's Star calls us to Him — and you.
    We'll seek Him, though it costs our very life.
    Seek you Him also; He's salvation's self.

Phares. Forty years Juda has borne the foreign yoke,
    And expectations thirsting for revenge
    Are strained, strained to the utmost they endure.
    He comes, His mantle red with heathen blood,
    He comes, His eyes with victory aglare,
    He comes, the battle-cry upon His lips;
    We seek Him — not if I do prize my life!

Balt. And Satan's yoke has Adam's mourning race
    Borne forty hundred years; from it to free us
    Cometh the gracious Saviour of the world.
    His kingdom's not from hence: and so hope not
    That He may claim an earthly crown — a Jew—
    He brings unto us all a heavenly crown.

Phares [*aloud*] People, would you desire to recognize
    A king of this degree?

All [*angrily*] No, never, no!

Kings and Nobles. Woe!

Phares. It is high time that we keep aloof
From you. The strength of a conspiracy
Makes you our danger.
    [*To the Multitude*] Citizens, we're off!
                  [*All flee. Exeunt.*]

SCENE VIII. The Same.

STROPHE I.

Balt. Jerusalem, Jerusalem, O City, God's delight,
Erewhile layest thou, the God-ruined, cursed,
I' the dust;
And wailing heardest thy ramparts,
With foes girded, beneath the battering
Of catapults crash and crumble, —
And wan, stark, sawest through the broken-down portals
Onrushing the surge of a wrathful sea,
Dread Nabuchodonosor's army.
Out, out hastened from amidst the gory devastation
Thy sons in shackles and thy daughters shamed and outraged;
Fearful, harried by the threatening falchions,
Moved they to the distant Euphrates' bank,—
Most desolate of peoples! —
To live as in a sepulchre.

ANTISTROPHE I.

All three Nobles Balt.
Wherefore flashed God enraged on Sion-town?

Dreading, shivering, listed we the ancients' narrative:
"If thou, O Jacob, abidest true,"
Thundered from Sinai's lightning-vested summit
The words of menace in our Araby's desert, —
"Unuttered blessings I now promise
Through all the land where milk and honey
flow, —
But if thou dare to revolt,
Execration followeth!"
The people swore their oath,
But foreign idol-worship, banquetting senseless, imbibed
And to foul Moloch's red-glowing arm in valley infernal
Whimpering children
Their parents
Cruelly submitted,
And the prophets' uplifted voice —
They drowned in the copious heart-streams.

Strophe II.

Gasp. When God His Only-begotten sendeth,
So frequently promised, so long expected,
The nations' blessing, Israel's peace,
Woe! Woe! Woe! Jerusalem, seekest thou not Him, as
we do,
Nor meetest Him in festival adornment?
Far from His boons, perennial fountain,
Turnest thou off, wicked,
With mind intoxicate, giddy, — far
From limpid floods of joy,
By gold enchantments ta'en thy heart, —

Far from truest riches' source?
Woe! thou'st consigned thy King to ignomy,
Slavish, crouching before the low tyrant, Antipater's son;
Although He comes to thee first to feel a world neglectful,
Wilt thou thy visiting God,
Like as the disinherited, thrust forth
From an ungracious threshold?

ANTISTROPHE II.

All three Nobles Gasp.
Ye tell me a bane, — the bane of rejection,
Ye city by-ways, evil, cold,
Till dashed to pieces Juda's pride I see:
Ay, as by a hurricane hurled to the dust,
Thou'lt, Juda, wrath in all climes undergo, —
It storms around thee, O monarchless,
Accursed, captive people!
The world's example, warning ever, thou,
Of a punishment and treason!

STROPHE III.

Melch.   His own received Him not — His own!
Us then, and you, who in the course of the centuries
Since the Saviour's advent bow to Him the knee,
O souls beyond our tale,
God hath, instead of
The Jewish stiffnecked race
As His own people chosen.

Antistrophe III.

All three Nobles Melch.
    Ye islands, countries, jubilation!
      Oh fashion us sons of God,
        Who may receive Him,
    O Only-begotten, O Son of God!

All.   Oh where, where shall we ever find Him?

Melch. Let's haste to the Temple now, for 'tis befitting,
    Obedient to a guardian hand,
  And pray 'twill lead us to the Christ unwitting
    And back again to fatherland.
          [*Exeunt omnes. The curtain falls.*]

ACT III.

SCENE I. JERUSALEM. Throne-room in Herod's palace. Darkness.

[*Enter Lucifer. Crosses the stage musingly.*]

Lucifer. I, Lucifer, I own the world's command!
Already men four thousand years have served;—
But now to rid me of my power o'er souls —
Ha! ha! — the great Messiah, dreaded oft,
Appears. Again as once in Heaven before
All time, — again as once on earth when time
Began, — again as through all time, I must
Use cunning, force. Ha! ha! — War to Thee, Messiah!
Herod shall be my faithfullest ally! [*Exit.*]

SCENE II. The Same.

[*Enter Herod and his Favorite, Cyrinus. Light.*]

Cyrin. The Arabs whom the toll-collector announced
I've found, praying within the Temple-gate.

Herod. What bent their steps to hitherwards?

Cyrin.   They would
Visit the new-born King, — ay, Juda's King!

Herod (*springing up*) Is then the One we long have hated come?

Cyrin.   So says the Star they saw in the East.

Herod (*aside, embracing throne*) Our throne! thou totterest,
  while lives this Child!
  (*Erect*) The common herd, have they th' intelligence?

Cyrin. Whoever came across their path, they asked him:
  "Pray, where is Juda's King?" a fearful phrase
  That in a trice filled all the town with fear. ...

Herod. And hope too, ever in the breast aglow.
  I am more eager than these foreigners
  To find the Saviour's rest. [*Thinks. Pause.*] Summon in haste
  The Priests — the Scribes likewise — unto our presence;
  They are the best to riddle mysteries.
  [*Exit Cyrinus.*]

SCENE III.   The Same.

[*Herod walks to and fro; stands before his throne.*]

Herod. O David's throne stolen from the Asmonean,
  Thou drippest with the blood of heroes moist
  Of our dear friends!   We do, methinks, espy
  Before thee sacrifices steeped in blood!
  Ay, look! the gray head of our bride's father,
  To us a very father. — Horrors dire!
  Our wife's corpse and our two sons' — together!
  How memory recalls the glance with which
  Dying ye sought a son's, a husband's, father's heart.
  But only one love knocked against this bosom,

And heaved it with anxiety — a love
That clutched Judea's crown, and hindered you
From robbing it yourselves, and cut you off;
Ay, ay, like to a tiger's dam, resenting
Each near approach, we watched our gory spoil.
[*Sits on throne; sways scepter.*]

Messiah, ha! The scepter of the Jew
Thou never shalt wrest from us. Our star shines still.
Soon as a babe Thou fall'st into our hands,
And eagerly we will strangle Thee, — convict
Of lie the Prophet who foretold that Thou
Enterest Jerusalem with royal state. [*Thinks.*]
A love-compelling Child—the Saviour—God!—
Our throne bestowed, recalled! — The fairy tales, —
No self-respecting Jew sets store by them! —
But if I do begin with a God's murder,
Then shall my downfall quickly move apace.

Lucifer [*from below*] Coward! Thy fancies set thy wits agog!

Herod [*leaping down*] What grewsome voice this, hot from lowest hell,
As though 'twas spoken by the demon-fiend,
Whose sway the Child too menaces with ruin!

Lucifer. Murder the new-born Babe and save thyself!

Herod [*after a space*] Th' advice is good, from whencesoe'er it comes.
O spright, I pray you tell where He is found

And I will... Hark! the sound of footsteps near!
Ha, ha! with cheerful brow's hypocrisy
We meet the basest of all hypocrites. [*Sits down.*]

SCENE VI. The Same.

[*Enter Ophni, the High priest, with the Sacred Text in hand; also several Scribes and Cyrinus. They prostrate themselves.*]

Ophni. As zephyrs sway the leaves, so every wish
Of yours swayeth us, O sovereign Majesty!
We're come obedient at your word in haste:
A goodly group of Priests and all the Scribes
Had thronged the hall of the Synedrion,
Deliberating how the deep unrest
Of people and of us alike may be
Assuaged, when lo! Cyrinus as despatched
By you to put the question in your name —
The question that disturbs Jerusalem;
And straight the answer as by miracle...

Herod. Where, where will Christ be born into the world?

Ophni. At Bethlehem, the royal Juda's hold!
Micheas' prophecy is a God-given
Assurance with regard to His birthplace...
List ye prophetic tones felicitous:
[*Unfolds scroll and reads.*]
"O Bethlehem of the Tribe of Juda, thou
Art not the least among the Princes of
Juda, for out of thee shall come the Leader
Who is to rule my people, Israel."

Herod. In Bethlehem bides this Prince of Israel.
  [*aside*] Ah, we have got Him in our clutches, now.
  [*To Cyrinus*] Cyrinus, thou bespeak these foreigners
    Once more, and when the mob are tired of gaping,
    'Twere best to fetch them home here to the Palace. [*Exit Cyrinus.*]

SCENE V. The Same.

Herod. "Thou Bethlehem of the Tribe of Juda!" Knew
  Ye then before that Christ springs from the Tribe
  Of Juda?

Ophni.   All Jews are well aware of it.
  When Josue first partitioned Chanaan
  The Princes of the Tribe of Juda claimed
  As their possession Bethlehem, where Jacob
  Buried his Rachel on the fatal birth
  Of Benjamin, her death : — a meager place —
  Its special glory's bruited far and near.
  For there Noemi walked and sought repose
  With the thrice faithful Ruth, who met her husband
  The while she gleaned the corn, Booz the good :
  Booz begat Obedom, Jesse's sire,
  From whom the Prophet-King, a Prophet's boast :
 [*From memory*] "A rod shall come from out of Jesse's root, —
    A flower shall rise up out of it. The Spirit
    Of God upon it shall abide. The root

THE THREE KINGS. 47

    Of Jesse stands on that day for a sign
    Unto all peoples, which they shall beseech."
    Of this world's Saviour, David, Jesse's son,
    Was the known figure. He, a shepherd bold
    At Bethlehem rent the lion and the wolf
    That robbed him of his sheep,—ay, he from Sion,
    Sion's noblest, guided the hosts of Israel.
    Thou City of David, oh the glory that
    Encircles thee! From thee springs David's Son
    Who shall be great: the Lord, as He assured
    David, shall place Him on His Father's throne
    To reign i' the house of Israel for aye.

Herod. Ye hypocrites, who the Messiah's Tribe
    And birthplace tell, yet dared with lying tongues
    To name us the Messiah — us though we be
    From Edom, Antipater's son.

Ophni [*aside*]   And so
    He wished himself, — the hypocrite! But what
    May I reply? [*goes to window, whence he sees Temple.*]
        O worthiest of Monarchs!
    Bethink the day on which we first did greet
    You as Messiah. Then you brilliant made
    The pageant of this Temple's consecration
    With numerous holocausts, and gained a glory
    Greater than Solomon. For you adorned
    The second Temple more than he the first,
    Albeit David's son, — and therefore we
    Beheld in you fulfilled Aggeus' word.

Herod [*breaking in*] Quick, read it!

Ophni [*reads*] "I will move the heavens and
 The earth, the sea and the dry land; and I
 Will move all nations: then, then the Desired
 Of all the nations shall appear."

Herod [*breaking in*] What sayest?
 We shall be he whom all — thou hypocrite! —
 Nations, and most of all the Jew, expect!
 Could we the confidence e'en of a small
 Kingdom conciliate by kindness or
 By force extort?

Scribe. Sire King, you have rebuilt
 Our Temple.

Herod [*to Ophni*] Give 's the prophecy entire.

Ophni [*reads*] "And I will fill this house with glory, saith
 The Lord of hosts: and great shall be the glory
 Of this last house more than of the first, saith
 The Lord of hosts."

Herod. You've torn this verse
 Out of its context and referred 't to us
 In liar's fashion. We've heard too the splendor
 Of the first Temple. Had we for the second
 Like David, treasures of large subject peoples,
 And skill like Solomon, prodigious skill?
 No, not a hundredth part! Ye have perverted
 The Scriptures, scoundrels all!
 [*Ophni droops his head.*]
 Read on some more!

Ophni [*reads*] "And in this place I will give peace."

THE THREE KINGS.

Herod. Through us
That sounds an ill-concealed reproof. No, War
And Murder are following, that aye
Accompany our every step unblessed.
[*points to Temple*] And when we reared upon the Temple gate
A stately golden Eagle, art's choice work,
The people murmured out aloud and spake:
"Th' abomination of the heathen set
I' the Holy Place." And if the likely time
Appear they'll surely rise and pull it down.
But I will burn the guilty every one.
[*To All*] Ye have essayed the worst that flattery
Dared, but a grave mischance has baffled you.
Ye've called us the Messiah, yet have read
For us that the Messiah comes not out
Of Idumea — no, but Bethlehem.
[*To the Scribes*] Avaunt ye liars! [*To Ophni*] Ophni, thou remain.

[*Exeunt Scribes abashed.*]

SCENE VI. The Same.

[*Herod walks to and fro restlessly, then eyes the Highpriest in anger; the Highpriest falls on his knees.*]

Ophni. O King, sire King! Your profit 'twas I sought
When I applied Aggeus' word to you.
Never could you the Jewish people win,
If they looked for salvation otherwhere.

Herod. But now can'st rivet their chain, although
Salvation's lit upon a graceless orb?

Ophni [*breathing freely*] I can, sire King. These Gentiles seek Him who
  Was born obscurely and unknown till now:
  We priests will not acknowledge Him before
  He comes attended to our Sion's Temple,
[*nodding to Herod significantly*]
  And there perhaps dire fate awaiteth Him.

Herod [*after a space*] Be 't so! Thou must cajole fanaticism
  At any cost. If unsuccessful, a
  Dire fate is thine. The Highpriest's Ephod we
  Have in a mighty tower to bestow
  On whomse'er we list — on Ananel
  Or on Aristobulus; one we called
  From Babylon despite your paper Law, —
  Th' other unexpectedly expired,
  When naked, bathing. Understandest thou
  Mine Highpriest, what we mean? Then useful be!
  [*Apart*] Ha, we might make these foreigners our tools!
  A plan, that soon will be developed!
  We're off to think it out. [*To the Highpriest*] An illness bids
  Us hence; thou entertain them till thou hearest
  A bell. Then shall Cyrinus lead them thence
  To royal feast, at which thou must attend them,
  He coming to our presence all alone.
  Beware thou ope thy lips on Bethlehem!

Ophni. I bide with the uncircumcised!

Herod. Slave, yes! [*Exit Herod.*]

SCENE VII. The Same.

[*The Highpriest rises from his knees and speaks, turned towards the door by which Herod departed.*]

Ophni. Ill-omened speech, "Where is the King of Jews?"
Unnerves your courage. Gentiles utter it, —
Oh shame!—And I must patient bear your mad
Fury until it do discharge itself!
Tyrant, th' avenger comes! Soon the Messiah
Shall end your sway and found theocracy,
A priestly rule; and you shall fawn upon
My feet e'en as I do upon your own!
O God of righteousness, make haste that I
May see the day of Edom's curse and gloat
In heartfelt glee o'er Edom's devastation!
[*Points out Palace*] Oh when, Messiah, when wilt Thou
    destroy
For now and aye this castled prison-rock?
[*Points out Temple*] When wilt Thou visit, Lord, Thy
    Temple's shrine?
When? Malachy the answer doth afford:
[*Declaims from memory*] "Behold, I send My Angel,
    and He shall
Prepare the way before My face. The Lord
Himself shall presently, — the Lord you seek,
The Angel of the Testament you do
Desire—shall come, shall come into His Temple.
Behold, He cometh, saith the Lord of Hosts.
Behold, before the coming of the great
Day of the Lord, I'll send to you Elias!"
And of the son of Zachary 'twas said

Within the Temple there: "And he shall go
Before Him in the spirit and power of
Elias." Sang not Zachary entranced
Words like Isaias', on the voice of one
Crying i' the wilderness? What shall this child
Become? Precursor? Angel? or Elias?
Already then the Saviour of the world is here.
A footfall that! I shall be silent, mum!

SCENE VIII. The Same.

[*Enter Levi Priest of Bethlehem; bows profoundly.*]

Levi. A greeting to the Highpriest! Long I've waited
I' the colonnade, till finally hither
I venture, where you bide, left by the King —
The presence-chamber open to the few —
To give the information that you wish.
Three hours ago all breathless hied to me
Your servant and his question put: "The Christ, —
The Christ, — is He yet born at Bethlehem?"
I stood and hesitated, doubting: Yes
Or No. I knew it and I know it not.
So I myself resolved to repair
To you and tell what recently transpired:
And 'tis my hope you'll extricate me from
The meshes of a fear that binds me fast.

Ophni. Let's hear! Be quick! The mere surmise that now
The rescue's near enchants me thoroughly.
[*Aside*] I'll feed upon this hope a space and still
My beating heart.

THE THREE KINGS. 53

Levi.   The sun hath forty times
Now risen, since Bethlehem was startled with
Th' announcement spread by shepherds that
    e'en then
The Saviour was born and heralded
By Angels' sheen and countenance supern.
To me and all the citizens these had
Seemed sensible until that hour, but when
They showed a Babe of lowly parents, — poor,
Who'd come to be enrolled and pay the tax, —
As Christ, we could accord them no belief.
After th' accustomed week the circumcision
Occurred. Us Joseph summoned, styled the
    father,
Whose mien a patriarchal dignity
Enhanced, that well beseemed him who would give
A name to the Most High ; and from his eyes
Shone forth a Seraph's love, that glowing served
And serving glowed. — Was he the Saviour's
    father?

Ophni. The Saviour no man shall beget : recall
    The words through David spoken: "Thou 'rt my
        Son, —
    This day I have begotten Thee!" And so
    The Saviour's Mother 'll not conceive of man.

Levi. [*as inspired*] The Mother of the Babe I saw, and were
    I then a Gentile, surely I had fallen
    In prostrate adoration. — Holy, heavenly!
    Her orbs lit with the purest luster that
    No breath e'er tarnished; her forehead clear

Bespoke her motherhood, and yet—Ah wonder!—
The rays she shed a virgin's honor claimed.
Ophni. Isaias of the Saviour's Mother spake:
"Behold a Virgin shall conceive and bear
A Son—she'll call His name Emmanuel!"
For God there's nothing that's impossible.
And Zachary in our own Temple at
The incense-altar heard the Angel tell,
His wife would have a child—a son of grace—
In her old age. And he was stricken dumb
For his distrust, until the child of grace
Was named, — a veritable John! — then loosed
His tongue in prophecy. So can our God's
Omnipotence o'ershadow her who bears
His Son.—Rain down, ye heavens, dew,—rain down
The just ye clouds. Open, O earth, and sprout Him.
Come, come Saviour, come! — But didst not say the Mother's
Poor?
Levi. Ay, yet hallowed grace encircled her
And them, most marvelous, so that when I
Gazed on the Babe—the fairest of mortals He!—
Methought I heard the Spirits bid: "Adore!"
Truly 'twas my opinion that a God
Had taken human flesh. Can God be clothed
In our habiliments of form and feature, —
In flesh, and bone, and blood,—and be both seen
And touched and loved by us?

Ophni.   He can forsooth:
Therefore the Saviour's name: "A God with us!"
Emmanuel can only be a God
With us, if He assume our nature, God
At once and man, and dwell upon the earth.

Levi. I relished, when began the circumcision,
The mystery of a God's presence near: —
The Babe appeared so God-like that he seemed
A Highpriest, with the Godhead unctuous, —
The Seed of Abraham in whom the nations
Will all be blessed, who made that day with God
Another covenant like to the one
The Patriarch first made: "A sacrifice
For mankind's sin, behold, — the body Thou'st
Given to Me," He seemed to say. God looked
With favor down upon the figure thus
Fulfilled and sealed with a so precious Blood!

Ophni. But what's the name?

Levi.   Ah, Jesus 'tis — Jesus!
Mary and Joseph, they gave it to Him, His
Blissful and blessed parents. When the Mother
Voiced it, the sound, as an ethereal music,
Gladdened the air, so passing sweet it was!

Ophni. He must for us be Jesus, Christ, and Saviour, —
Destroy all evil and obtain all good!

Levi. Can then a Babe the great Messiah be?

Ophni. In sooth. But where's the Babe?

Levi.   I found Him in
A manger. . . .

Ophni. [*Infuriate*] How! what! Emmanuel, great High-
 priest,
 This Temple's boast, and in a manger laid!
 In a foul manger the Establisher
 Of our theocracy! Thou hadst a fever
 And midst thy wanderings deceived thy sense.
 Hence, off! out of my sight, and if thou value
 Thy post, be circumspect.

Levi. [*falling on his knees*] Forgiveness! but
 I cannot rid me of these troubling thoughts:
 Hereafter I will treat them as a brood
 Of ill — [*aside*] to hold your favor and my bread!
 [*Exit.*]

SCENE IX. The Same.

Ophni. A stable owns Him, couched the beasts among!
 'Twere fitter far to see Him thence forsooth
 And to confess Him Saviour only when
 The day of doom shall break upon the world.
 The scepter's lost, yet He is not come to free us!
[*Goes to window and points the Temple, holding Bible in left
 hand.*]
 This Temple He is yet to visit and
 With immolations, teachings, miracles,
 Proclaim Himself right gloriously — God.
 "There only shall we find Him whom we seek,
 The Angel of the Testament we do
 Desire." I hope so long as this His Temple
 Graceth the crest of Sion: if it fall,
 Ah then, O Israel, oh yield to despair!

SCENE X. The Same.

[*Enter Cyrinus with Three Kings and their Retinue; they move slowly, but he hurries to the Highpriest.*]

Cyrin. Highpriest, the King's not here! Where is the King?

Ophni. He's in the Palace somewhere; 'twas an illness
Called him away. [*Low*] Soon he'll a signal give,
Until then only thou shalt be host to these,
              [*Points with scorn to the Kings.*]
Straightway to go to him thyself alone.

Cyrin. [*Aside*] He's studied well the craft of policy.
[*To the Kings*] Before you stands the Highpriest of the Jews.
              [*All three bow profoundly.*]

Gasp. [*approaching*] You are the true God's Highpriest worthy high
Esteem and high renown! Good fortune's brought
Us hither, you can best the answer tender
To our question! — An oracle speaks by
Your lips. — Where is the new-born King of Jews?
We saw His Star e'en in the Orient
And we have come Him to adore.

Ophni. [*Aside*]   What shame
These words are freighted with for me to-day!
[*Scornfully to the Kings*] Ye saw His Star e'en in the Orient?
To you then at a distance rather than
To us in His own Temple — Ay, to you
Th' uncircumcised rather than to us, His own

Who serve His Sanctuary and His Chosen
People,—hath God the Father deigned to
Reveal, that Juda's King has now been born?
No! no! Ye superstitious star-gazers, —
Ye blaspheme God! [*Rends his garment*] Yes, a
    will-o'-the-wisp
Out of the hellish swamp drives you, Magicians,
Wrong, — and an evil spirit's led you here
To cause Jerusalem worry, anguish and
Disheartenment. Ah! Free our city from
Your presence drear, that minds us of the grave's
Sheet-covered spooks.

All.   Ah! ah! woe! woe!

Gasp.   O Priest
Revered, our eyes beheld the Star!

All [*with uplifted hands*]   We swear 't!

Gasp. And inly in our heart sounded: "This is
The Star of Balaam!"

Balt.   Sure, Jacob's Star
Your own most sacred Book foretells!

Ophni [*pointing to Temple*]   But Christ
Comes with magnificence into His Temple,
To rear a proud theocracy anew
And to perform what prodigies we ask ; —
Else we will never recognize Him.

All   Woe!

Melch. Now we appreciate the words of menace
With which the prophets one and all denounced

That finally you'd be rejected. — Hope,
Hope still, companions; God shall shelter us!
A honied speech falls from th' inspired mouth,—
And to our interest: "Oh jubilee,
Ye Gentiles, He hath drawn from you His kingdom!"

Strophe I.

[The Highpriest and Cyrinus remain mute with wonder during the rest of the scene. Baltassar beholds the Bible on the table and approaches thither.]

Balt. What bids me inly to the Book of Prophecy?
O faith of God supern, whose treasured words by Him
Within a scroll enclosed here lie,
[Kneels, kisses the Book and venerates it.]
Come, ope my orbs, illumine what is dim!
[Reads from Isaias, XLII, 6 and 7.]
"I have now elected Thee — elected
And ta'en Thee by the hand securely,
And made Thee by my folk respected,
A light to th' Heathen!
That to the blind their vision surely
And to the captive freedom thou'dst restore
Hid in the prison-barrack, wreathen
With deepest horrors, nevermore!"
[Raises eyes to Heaven.]
Shine forth, O Star, O light, and the Maker of earth portend
And lead where grace and submission blend
Most beauteously from end to end!

ANTISTROPHE I.

All three Nobles Balt.

    Jehova's finger chiseled
    The Law on the olden stone
Which He from Sinai's height in Araby's bleak
        desert to Israel gave,
    While the thunderbolts sizzled:
And Thou, Thou, O Founder of a world-alliance,
    Writest in flaming letters
    A love that's alone,
    On our hearts; — we're Thy debtors; —
Ah, may the glare of Thy Star and the thrill of
        its joyance
    Us in the latter day save!

STROPHE II.

Gasp.   Through sweetest constraint
    Heed I the power
    Attractive towards the priceless dower
    Of wisdom enshrined 'neath pages so quaint:
[*Takes scroll from Baltassar, venerates it and reads:*]
    "I take no pleasure from the heartless sacrifices,"
    How sternly speaks the Lord of hosts!
    "Out of your hand the gift no more will I accept,
For from the very moment the Sun imperial rises,
    E'en to his setting,
    Now 'mong the Heathen
    Through every land the prayer uprises,
And there is offered in My Name a clean oblation
The gladdest honors showing, with gladsome
        honors wreathen, —
    Now 'mong the Heathen!

[*Looks up to Heaven*] O Star we have wept, —
    O oracle, — the habitation
    Where thankful creation
Long adoreth,—where He the All-Holy hath slept,
    The Victim that boasts
    A priest from every nation!

Antistrophe II.

All three Nobles Gasp.
    Levi, faithless Tribe, draws direst curses
        Abundant down,
    As blemished holocaust reverses
    Th' Almighty's benignant intention, —
        On Temple and town.
    Breaking covenants, he quakes
'Fore the Father of the Future he makes
        Dread Judge of the earth:
But soon shall he feel in his vitals a fiery birth,
        And the dried expansion
    And the root of his barren tree
        Desolated shall be!
Methinks I now hear the praises of an offering of
        bread and wine; —
Melchisedech, Salem's own Monarch and Priest,
That offering so welcome and holy was thine, —
    The other has ceased.
    And Thou whom we're seeking,
Christ, Thou art of Melchisedech's order,
        Designed for eternity's power!
O offering liberal, created border

O'erstepping, the sun Thou greetest, a dower
Myriads of altars display, not now reeking
With blood,—and a God smiles mercy from Thee,
And Thou causest the demons to cower,
    Good men Heaven to see!

Strophe III.

Melch. Ah, sweetly resoundeth a mandate:
"Take the scroll and read!" [*He goes to Gaspar, venerates the Holy Writings, raises them to his lips, kisses them, finally drops them quickly and exclaims:*]

O wonder open to mine eyesight!
A newer star displayeth here!
[*Reads inspiringly Ps. LXXX, 10.*]
"The Monarchs of both Tharsis and the Islands,
    E'en they shall present their offerings, —
The Monarchs of the Arabs and of Saba,
    E'en they to Him gifts shall carry, —
Adore all the Monarchs of the nations
And all the peoples bow to Him!"

[*In a sublime elevation.*]

Beheld us the glance of the Psalmist prophetic,
    Prostrate before our God-King kneel!
Whom we now anxious are seeking, —
Whom we shall in gladsomeness find.

Antistrophe III.

Gasp. and Balt. Us sang the Royal Singer God-enlightened!

All.   Of us spoke heavenly his harp-chords!
Our bosoms well forth thanks to Thee, O God!
Thy vision hath us eternally discerned,

Thou'st summoned us from far off oceans hither
Our homage to pay
To the Emmanuel-God!
[*All kneel with the exception of the Highpriest.*]

Melch. [*with eyes and hands raised*]
To Thee, O joyous Lord, who rulest with the joyous fulness
From sea to sea and to the earth's confines,
Ere that the moonlight disappear
Lead us through mazy labyrinths
To Thee!

[*Bell sounds. Cyrinus conducts them to the door through which Herod departed. The Highpriest moves disturbed to the other side.*]
[*Curtain falls.*]

ACT IV.

SCENE I. Jerusalem. Secret apartment in Palace of King Herod. Herod in deep thought on his throne.

[*Enter Cyrinus.*]

Cyrin. Great King, the foreigners, as you have bidden
I've kept in lieu of yourself right splendidly.

Herod. What think'st of them?

Cyrin. They're wise in word and deed,
And surely higher inspiration guides
Their steps.

Herod. A star and oracle!

Cyrin. In sooth;
Th' invisible profound has broken its silence
And will make public that a God hath crossed
Its limits to dwell with mankind. Astounded
Wonder hath seized upon my soul at what
My friend Romanus, the philosopher,
Arrived today from Rome, details of the
Messiah.

Herod. Haste and call him; I would hear. [*Exit Cyrinus.*]

SCENE II. The Same. Herod at a table.

Herod. No hesitation: the Messiah is come.
Our plan is now evolved. Ha, Arabs, ye

Shall pay your due to death and hold your tongue.
We'll compass it on your return : till then
Act as our tools, out pliant instruments,
> [*Stands up, raises his clenched hand.*]

That we may find this new-born King of Jews.
And when we find, Thou'rt consigned to doom,—
To doom, our worthy New-born, to no throne!
> [*Walks to and fro.*]

'Twere foul to use deceit and lies with strangers!
Bah! Politics acknowledges for virtue
Hypocrisy. — But if our craft do fail?
Right often Fortune's blight destroyeth us: —
We must prepare for all contingencies.
Succeed we — good; succeed we not, we'll try
Some other means : albeit which, if they
Elude us? [*Thinks*] Then we'll murder every babe
In Bethlehem's environment, and He
Shall not be able to escape the steel. [*Sits down*]
Can aught come of this blood-immersed thought?
Naught! Babes! So innocent, defenseless, weak!

[*An unearthly voice from below*]

Lucifer. A plague on them, provided thou art rid
Of Him thou dreadest, that Messiah-King!

Herod. The lower world is clearly prompting us.
> [*Springs up shrieking, then pauses to think.*]

What harm if it be right : we must kill all!
> [*Looks to the side.*]

Cyrinus comes: now bide thee mighty still.

SCENE III. The Same.

[*Enter Cyrnus with Romanus.*]

Cyrin. A hail to Herod!

Herod.   This countenance we have
Beheld somewhere, but where we cannot say.

Rom.   Among the gormandizing club of Marcus
Antonius.

Herod.   Ah yes, yes, at Rome full eight
And thirty years ago, when he the crown
Of Israel on us bestowed in state
From Jupiter's high altar. Thankful we
To Jupiter and to Apollo both
Builded a temple. Know, we still revere
Them honorably.[*Points out to two statues in the room.*]
            Where hast thou lived since?

Rom.   The latest at Augustus' court, as he
A noble furtherer of learning and
Belles-lettres, had invited me to hold
My place within the circle of his friends!

Herod What think ye there of the Messiah's advent?

Rom.   The expectation of preceding ages
Hath reached its highest pitch here in our own:
And Cicero, of orators the prince,
The best of statesmen, with a host of others
Long speak of Him. Most recently however
Virgil, than whom there never sang a poet
Of loftier conception, gave to me, —
Ay, gave into this hand, — a copy of
His Eclogue, prepossessing all men's hearts,
Wherein he speaks, as though that were fulfilled,
Which the Cumean Sibyl, one of nine,
Did manifest regarding Him, our Hope.

THE THREE KINGS. 67

Herod. We would drink in those strains as fast as e'er
      We may.

Rom.   I read them. — O thou jewel of
                    [*Takes slip from under his toga.*]
      My heart! — "The time appointed by the lay
      Of Cuma's Sibyl now at last hath come:
      Already larger now the months around
      Their dizzy orbits whirl. The Virgin's come!
      The age of Saturn hath returned, and brings
      From heavenly spheres the progeny supern!"
                    [*Turns slip and proceeds.*]
      He treats also the golden reign of Christ:
      "And our transgressions, if they still remain
      In their effects, He'll cure, — and free the earth
      From ceaseless dread. The Child shall lead a life
      Divine, and rule the universe in joy.
      No more the herds quail at the lion's roar:
      The poisoned plant, the serpent dire, succumb."

Cyrin. So issues from a heathen pen th' inspired
      Isaias' prophecy.

Herod.   At Rome they too
      Await the coming of the Christ.

Rom.   If He's
      At all to come and save mankind, He must
      Come now: For great the need of Him. In shades
      Of death, — in midnight darkness as of hell, —
      We lurk. And though creation beams upon
      Us knowledge of our God, th' inhabitants
      Of earth by millions drown within a marsh
      Of sins the living spark. E'en his own hand

Hath writ the law upon our hearts, yet none
Obey, — none feel the import of His words.
All wickedness is deified, and crimes
Are lauded : avarice, lust, blood, excess
And perfidy are venerated with
The foulest practices.   Unless He haste
And draw the world to other courses, teach
To know our God, to love fair virtue's grace,
Mankind are warranted in the belief
That there is not a Saviour promised them.

Herod. This Saviour, — where shall He appear?

Rom. The Chinese
Confucius said to his Easterners :
"In Western lands Salvation shall you find."
And pole to pole in every clime resounds
The ancient prophecy: "From Juda hope
Alleviation of our race's woe."

Herod. Then the idea that a Saviour comes
Hath conquered Rome, with Rome the world, and started
Vice from its vile enjoyments ; and apace
Is disaffection spreading 'mong the Jews.
That minds me of Aggeus whom the Highpriest
Hath quoted : "I will move the heavens and
The earth, the sea and the dry land,— and I
Will move all nations : then, then the Desired
Of all the nations shall appear."

Rom. Under
Augustus God hath moved the earth and sea

In battle for a universal sway
Until all lands, with paean-shouts replete,
The third time since the founding of the City,
Have heard that Janus' door of peace is shut,
And people stream to be enrolled by
The Prefects of Augustus.

Cyrin.   Ay, forsooth
A strange convulsion's seized on nature now:
But lately Angels left a blissful Heaven's
Rest, coming to the Temple here in hosts
From Nazareth and Bethlehem. — So speaks
The vulgar rumor.

Rom.   Rome, around the sun —
It was serenest noon — three rings of light
Beheld and then a golden ball borne down
Through th' azure depths. And likewise to
        Augustus
In dreams appeared a Virgin and her Child;
Who thereupon did raise an altar in
His Palace: "To the God, God's only Son."
God's only Son, the Virgin's Son, is our
True friend, — His Name is as the oil poured
        forth :
Yea, there did flow in Rome for one whole day
A spring-stream of the purest oil. Besides
He is the enemy of plural gods:
They all pay fearing homage to Him. And
Delphi is silenced, and the Capitol
Yields up the idols of all peoples, struck
By lightning. Jupiter, the thunderer,
Is fall'n.

Herod.   Before His coming trembles earth
      And heaven; like my throne shake the thrones
          of gods.

Cyrin. And as His harbinger to the far East
      A Star was from the starry millions sent....

Herod. Fomenting discord and proclaiming news
      That causes worry to Jerusalem
      And us!

Rom.   From Rome came I to Sion's walls,
      Impelled by an unconquerable woe
      And longing to desert dark heathendom
      And hie to light, to faith, to truth, and love:—
      And now the wondrous word prophetical
      Aggeus uttered is fulfilled. The Saviour
      Hath come, — hath surely come! [*Turns towards statues of Jupiter and Apollo; then with his hand upraised.*]
                          Ye idols vain,
      I do forswear you! I renounce the world
      And sin and Satan! I believe in the
      One only God, assenting now beforehand
      To whatsoever Christ may teach. — This trust
      I carry back with me to Rome in peace.
                                 [*Bows. Exit.*]

Herod. Cyrinus, haste you, get those foreigners!
      Hark, fetch a copy of the Scriptures too.
                               [*Exit Cyrinus.*]

SCENE IV. The Same.

[*The two statues with a crumbling rattle fall to pieces.*]

Herod. [*Shrieks in his blind fnry.*] Messiah, Thou wilt
have no gods besides Thee!
Ha, Thou art dangerous to our cherished hopes!
And Hades, all excitement, urgeth us
To enter into giant-war with Thee. [*Turns towards the broken fragments.*]
We swear it by these fragments once of gods,—
Thou diest! And if in Bethlehem the trio
Among the bratlings find Thee not, they all
Shall tumble o'er the brink of life
Into the precipice of death, so Thou with them
Relinquish earth. [*Thinks, then after an interval*]
What was His age? His age—
We'll reckon it from the appearance of
The Star: that will be near enough, we judge.
[*Again thinks, and again after an interval.*]
But numbers hardly show the likely growth.—
An executing legion, if they had
To force the homes and put the question
To parents, would consume long hours and days.
We add two years to the presumed time
And order all the young ones born within
The past two years to death. The tax-list
knows them:
They shall not break the meshes of this net.
[*Covers fragments.*]

SCENE V. The same.

[Enter Cyrinus and the Three Kings: looks inquiringly at the empty pedestals, and the covered fragments; a glance from Herod puts him on his guard.]

Melch. [*greets Herod, while the others bow.*]
 We greet you, Herod, Lord of Juda's land!
 Where lies the new-born King? We saw His Star
 E'en in the farthest regions of the East,
 And hither we have come, Him to adore.

Herod. Ne'er did the magic wand more truly tell
 The spot than we with but a word.

All [*thronging round him with longing intent.*] So you
 Know where He is, the Saviour whom we seek?

Herod. This is the Book of God. Micheas speaks: [*Reads.*]
 "O Bethlehem of the Tribe of Juda, thou
 Art not the least among the Princes of
 Juda, for out of thee shall come the Leader
 Who is to rule my people, Israel, —
 Whose going forth is from the days of an
 Eternity." [*Gives Book back to Cyrinus.*]
  In Bethlehem, a place
 Of small extent, to the Southwest two miles
 From here, is found the Jewish King you want.

All [*falling on their knees.*] In Bethlehem, in Bethlehem!
 thank God!

Melch. [*with hands outstretched and eyes raised to Heaven.*]
 We thank Thee, Spirit of the Lord, for giving
 To us an oracle most unexpected, —
 The long-sought answer to the question that
 We oft put ineffectually.

Balt. O
 Father above, all thanks: from Thee this word.
 This holy inspiration is diffused!

Gasp. A star of joy illumed the night, by anguish
 Riven, and led us to the Son of God.

All [*rising*] Let's off! To Bethlehem! To Bethlehem!
 [*They are about to go.*]

Herod. Hold! Tell me first when you espied the Star!

Melch. 'Tis now a moon, since we did undertake,
 Three friends, this holy journeying;
 Twelve days before that we espied the Star.

Herod. Is this th' exact account of its appearance?

Melch. Ay.

Herod [*to Balt. and Gasp.*] Hath your friend in nothing
 erred?

Balt. and Gasp. In nothing.

Herod [*to the others.*] Is 't as he hath pronounced?

All Nobles. It is forsooth.

Herod. When twelve days old ...

Gasp. [*interrupts Herod.*] O ye twelve days in which
 Th' Eternal's lived concealed on the earth,
 Be henceforth sacred!

Herod. How can you Him name
 Eternal, who knows but forty days.

Gasp. Of Him
 Micheas said, as you explained to us:
 "His going forth is from the days of an

Eternity." [*Then in ecstasy.*] In the beginning was
The Word; the Word was God: the Father Him
Begot long ere the morning star, His Son,
In the to-day of His eternity:
This Word hath taken flesh.

All [*genuflecting.*]   And dwelt amongst us.

Balt. [*In a loftier strain.*] Thou art the fulness of all time, Christ's birthday!
In Eden, changed then to grief, the Sire
Of our doomed race expected thee and joyed
Four thousand years ago; and when sin caused
The deluge in the midst of a great era,
Noah three thousand years ago did look
To thee, as did the faithful Abraham
Two thousand years ago; and in the desert
Moses prayed fifteen hundred years ago
For thee; of thee sang David a thousand years
Ago, and Daniel five hundred years
Ago, — his seventy weeks of years. Thou art
For Rome the day of mightiest happiness
That hath within seven centuries and a half
Appeared since her establishment, the two
And fortieth year of the first Emperor,
Augustus.

All three Nobles Balt. O thou day, salvation-laden
For Jews and Gentiles! In thee goes forth the Light
That shall enlighten every man that comes
Into the world.

THE THREE KINGS.

Melch. [*In prophetic rapture.*] Christ's birth! The central point
 Of all our time, to thee the centuries
 Converge: the world before thee looked to thee
 With Hope, and coming ages shall look back
 In thankfulness to thee. The life our Lord
 On thee begins is as the progress grand
 Of a sun and shall denote the festive time,
 The hour of prayer. The glories of the rule
 That He shall found, — ay, its vicissitudes,
 Shall mark the turning point of history:
 And He directs it; e'en the future read
 His searching eyes, — to us a mystic book
 With seven seals secured. But lo! the war
 Is done — the Last Day's come. O Judge, appear!
 Of epochs the beginning and the end,
 And lead to bliss who honors Thee, and thrust
 Into the everlasting night Thy foes, —
 O Thou enduring center of all time, —
 And haste to consecrate to Thee, the days,
 The hours of this our earthly pilgrimage.

All three Nobles Melch.
 At Bethlehem, the House of Bread, far richer
 Than the Egyptian Joseph's granaries,
 Supplied with an abundance for the world,
 We find a bread, a manna, fallen from Heaven,
 Productive of immortal life and vigor.

All. We're off! To Bethlehem! To Bethlehem!

Herod. So go to Bethlehem and diligently
Search for the Child ; whom when you've found,
Come hither back and let us know, that we
May also render Him the homage due.

Gasp. Herod, you are the Saviour's instrument:
Through you He's brought us prosperous to Him.

Herod. Seek accurately and when you've got Him,
Acquaint us that we too may faithfully
Adore — [*Goes off muttering*] or rather rid ourselves of Him.   [*Exit Herod.*]

SCENE VI. The Same.

Melch. Caught ye the man's concluding muttered speech.

All. No.

Melch. Well, his mutterings have pierced our soul
With fear. It seems as if grinned Satan from
His countenance, and showed that he is
What the people say he is — the enemy
Of the Messiah. Therefore sinister
He plans, but he is foiled, as be they all
That ever dare to wage a war 'gainst God.

STROPHE I.

Melch.

The Eternal Father commanded the lords of His regions,
  "Honor the Eternal Word,

THE THREE KINGS.

 Who flesh in the fulness of time is given!"
Then Lucifer haughtily averred:
"No!
Over the stars erect I a peerless throne
To be alone!"
Spake he, and led 'gainst th' Almighty a woe-begetting assault in Heaven,
The war of the demons with Michael's legions.

ANTISTROPHE I.

All three Nobles Melch.
"Who is like God!"
Loud rang the battlecry through the endless expanses,
And lightning-confounded
They suddenly bounded
Into nethermost brimstone, — angelic lances
By millions, deceived
Of Satan fondly believed, —
The princes of darkness a-weltering there with gloomiest terror surrounded
And conscience's prod.

STROPHE II.

Gasp.
Standing on th' historic Red Sea's border,
Looking o'er its billowy vast disorder,
In my awestruck soul I felt,
Strange, a prophetic start:
Under bleached the ancient corses

           Of the Egyptian and his horses,
    Who dared the people of God to menace with
               murder :
         "Let go My people!"   He did not melt,
         But rather hardened his heart.

Antistrophe II.

All three Nobles Gasp.
         And when the Jews 'tween liquid walls sought
               the Asian coast,
    Rashly he dared to attempt the yawning abyss with
               a boast ;
               But mid the dreadfullest louring,
                Shut them those jaws, devouring
         Horse and chariot and king and host.

Strophe III.

Balt.
               Right many the powers that harrassed
                    Jehovah's people :
         Shuddering bethought I its unhappy lot,
    When lo!   Ninive's ruin and Babylon's saw I:
    And I rehearsed all the world-rulers' falls,
    Glancing mine eye 'long the vistas of time
         E'en to the Antichrist's day. —
    Oh wherefore conspire ye 'gainst the Christ,
         Ye mighty of earth?
              Jehovah — mocks your efforts ;
         Unimpeachable bides His resolve :
              "My Son art Thou, My Messiah,

Worldwide be Thy domain;
With iron-shod scepter coerce all Thy en'mies
And dash them to pieces like earthenware vessels!"

ANTISTROPHE III.

All three Nobles Balt.

O Kings of the dynasties in future!
Give hearing to those massive relics:
"Try not with metal and folly
The King of the ages to conquer,
Who is wont the haughty to disenthrone!"

All Nobles.

Now let us, O Kings, with a joy-winged speed to our feet assemble
To our Saviour and King,
The Saviour anointed!

All Three Kings.

We bow before the Lord, whose day
Divine is fixed for ever and aye.

[*Curtain falls.*]

ACT V.

SCENE I. Sunset. The road half way to Bethlehem lying to the Southwest. A moss-covered stone-bench.

[*Enter the Three Holy Kings with their companions. The Star suddenly appears. Goes from one side to the other before them. They are dumbfounded and look at it most intently.*]

All.   Oh! Oh!!

Gasp.   The Star!

Balt.   O Jacob's Star!

Melch.   The Star's Appeared again!

Balt.   Oh fortune truly great!

Melch.   Oh blessedness!

Gasp.   Its ray streams heaving grace Into our hearts!

All.   Oh! Oh!!

Melch. [*to the Star*]   Thou, spirit of God, Movest lighting us before. We'll find the Christ!

Balt. [*to the Star*] Thou, Angel, shinest on our way to Him!

Gasp. [*to the Star*] Thou, Saviour's Star, directest right to Him!

All.   Oh! Oh!!

Melch.   O God's paternal love!

Balt.   Secure
We hope, we joy!

Gasp.   A jubilee more sweet
Than when at first we saw thee shine entranced!
                        [*All set themselves in motion.*]

Balt. We'll follow thee!

Melch.   Our sorrow is turned now
To victory!

Gasp.   Oh! Oh!! We triumph!

All.   Oh!!! [*Exeunt omnes.*]

SCENE II. The Same.

[*Enter Herod disguised as a private citizen. He stares in the direction along which the Star has disappeared.*]

Herod. Woe to thee, Herod! Woe, where hast thou fled?
Where every star-beam lights a hellish fire
Within thy bosom,—gaze no more, O eyes!
The blinding of its sheen inspires new fears.
                        [*Turns all round.*]
Woe to unhappy us! Like Cain bemoaning
His brother's murder, we can find no rest
Under th' o'erstretching vault of God, our foe.
                        [*Points to Palace.*]
Within our Palace dwell unnumbered sprites,
That dreadful howl: "Thou art forever ours!"
How tingle their taunts of mockery in our ears,
Chilling the marrow of our bones! We've fled
Hither to have some respite: here a star

Is threatening,—the baneful Star,—our death.
[Looks out over the country: then sits on the bench.]
'Tis gone: good, here therefore we may repose
A while, for we have long lacked all repose.
Shall we associate with yonder folk?
The walk would lead to a most pleasant knoll:
But nay! We must proceed in secrecy
When round us bristle not the awing spears
Of hired guards. And well might they discern
'Neath falsifying raiment who we are, —
To glad our subjects with the news: "He's slain!"
And should we not be recognized, no words
Of benediction shall attend our steps.
[Turns towards Jerusalem and speaks looking up at his Palace.]
The whole world hates us! Fell conspiracy
Lurches within our family circle. And
Suspicion galls our food. Ay, if our heir
Embraces with his left, we shun his right,
Lest it may plunge a dagger in our breast.
[Clenches his fist.]
Son, thou wouldst fill our throne before the time,
Yielding no more to us, than owns a swine
Within its pen, — Augustus' precious boon.
Thou must be taught a lesson ere we die.
Woe! woe! A worm is gnawing at our soul!
That we might drown our conscience all in blood!
A worm it is, with venom sting, — and robs
Us night and day of peace. Eternal scourge
Of evil life, eternal threatening! *[Looks down.]*
And the dumb earth itself is shouting Heavenward

For vengeance 'gainst us with its myriad tongues,
 As corpses gird it round, our deed, begrimed
 With gore, which it in mercy doth absorb.
 How oft we've reddened it out of the veins
 Of th' innocent,—moistened it with their tears.
 But at the hour of midnight we with moans
 And horrors and death-rattlings are beset
 And prowling blanched specters point at us.
   [Raises his voice.]
Will not the murder of a harmless babe, —
 Christ's murder,—swell their rage a hundredfold?
   [Stands up.]
Unhappy we! To what ascribe these woes?
 Usurped scepter of the Jew, thou art
 An iron rod that fate e'er heavily
 Lays on! Thou throne of Israel, how hard
 Thy circlet sits upon a stranger head!
 With gripe of iron dullest thou our sense,
 Upon our forehead placed. But yet 'tis sweet:
 "Herod, the mighty Monarch of the Jews!"
 And though we inwardly the witness bear:
 "Scoundrel, the mighty robber of the Jews,
 The Judge of Kings shall pay thee back in kind!"
 We can't relinquish what we now possess.
   [Turns towards Bethlehem.]
There bides to Whom belongs this land and crown
 By right — the new-born King of Juda — Ha!
 Like any other child He careless there
 Laughs in the smile of an own Mother's love.
 Messiah, Juda's King, Thou must succumb!
 And if these foreigners display Thee not,

Then every suckling under two years old
Within th' environs shall succumb with Thee.
[*A thunder-clap. Herod sinks as though stricken by lightning.*]

SCENE III. The Same.

[*Enter Cyrinus quickly.*]

Cyrin. Sire King! O Herod! I, your truest friend,
Have followed you in secret that I might
Be near to aid. What is it that's occurred?
[*Looks at him and flees.*]
Alas! alas! the anger of the Lord
Sits hard upon him: I will never more
Be his attendant.

Herod [*calls after him*] Thou, thou also, whom
We thought a constant friend, desertest us?
[*Exit Cyrinus.*]

SCENE IV. The Same.

[*Herod sits down on the bench.*]

Herod.

Alas! alas! alas! a sword
That runneth through flesh and bone
Into the quick!
We are weakened all!
Our sinews — of vigor they are
Bereft, — they're scattered!
What pain in every joint!
About our heart
The blood is congealing,
And from our breast we feel buoyed up
The air of corruption!

Alas! alas! vengeance divine to death
    Hath now devoted us!
Alas! His might hath wrought dire disease,
    And henceforth we die
A lingering death, full of anguish, of grief!
    We pine a very corpse,
    Living a sepulchre!
Alas! alas! how fierce it gnaws at our flesh!
    What penetrates
    Into our bosom?

[*Tears open his tunic, looks in, then springs up shrieking.*]
    Worms!!
    Worms swallow us whole!
    Dreadfullest God!
Thy condemnation sounds within our ears:
"Death in lieu of life shalt live, worm-eaten;
Worms from the grave consume him entire!"

Lucifer [*from below.*]   Thou art mine!
Here now awaiteth thee a hellish dragon,—
    The worm never-dying!
    Thou art forever mine.

Herod.   Woe! woe! Alas! [*Flees. Exit.*]

SCENE V. The Same.

(The following visions, where it is possible, ought to be shown by means of stage illusions with mirrors.)

[*Enter the Holy Simeon; he looks towards Heaven.*]

Simeon. O Spirit of God that soft impels me on!
"Thou shalt not see thy death, until thou seest
Th' Anointed of the Lord," Thou said'st to me;

And but to-day I saw the Temple's Glory;
The God-like beauteous Child was thither
    brought,
While in her hand the Mother showed a poor
Offering of doves.—'Twas Mary! Well I knew
    her,
Before she was espoused to Joseph there.
My joy supreme; though it waxed far intenser,
When the Gentiles' question stirred Jerusalem:
"Where is the King, your Juda's new-born King?
We saw his Star shine in the Orient."
Their eyes yearn for Salvation's vision,
Which Thou'st prepared before the eyes of
    mortals,
A Light unto th' illumining of Heathens.
Yet now my heart is steeped in very dread
For the Child Jesus' sake, and it renews
Petitions for the grace to die i' the Lord.
Herod will persecute this tender One;
And Mary's heart soon will the sword-thrust
    drink:
Already is the Lamb of God a victim?

Voice of God [*from above*] Hark, Simeon! hark, Simeon!

Simeon.   O Lord!
    Here am I: speak, Lord, for Thy servant
        heareth!

Voice of God. View Bethlehem! what seest thou, son
    of man?

Simeon [*looks towards Bethlehem.*] Woe! what relentless
    tyrant's rage let loose

THE THREE KINGS.

Heaps murdered victims everywhere within
Th' environs sanctified of Bethlehem.
Here slumbers in its crib an only child
Of a young parent : cold the dagger's point
Doth probe its heart, and shrieking she falls, pale
As death, upon the corpse that stains with blood
The clothes in which she decked her darling one.
There, where a brother's and a sister's hands
Direct the tottering steps now first essayed,
A brand gleams suddenly and with dire wound
Baffles the joy that love so fond conceived;
While she whole flesh that is, whose blood, whose bone,
Is petrified, and stays, — the feebler rest
Have gone! They tear the precious burden from
A weaponless embrace that would defend
A first-born son. But weakness has to yield
Before the strength of brawny muscles, eager
To perpetrate the murder of a babe.
His breast is riven and quivering he gasps
His last, more firmly held in that embrace,
Though changed so piteously! There bloody lie
Upon the threshold of a house four, two
Are old, two young—the lance hath pierced them all!
From Rama and from Bethlehem, where died
Rachel, as Benjamin in sorrow she
Did bear, is heard a voice of lamentation
And mourning — Rachel wails her children now
Nor will she hearken aught to comfort, for

Cruel Murder's torn the loved ones from her soul
And quelled them in the silence of the tomb.
    [*Lifts his eyes to Heaven. Pause.*]
Oh, there before God's throne the martyrs play!
    [*Short pause; looks to the South.*]
Within a hut that palms o'erspread there rests
The God-like beauteous Child; His Mother kneels
In adoration near, and lo! above
An Angel hovereth to tell the Father
In sleep: "Return to Israel; they are
All dead, who wish to slay the Child Divine."
    [*Short pause.*]
In Nazareth's small town the Child Divine
Grows up within the Holy Family.
    [*Short pause; looks to the West.*]
Lo! High in air angelic double choirs,
Singing their lays alternately, appear
And Westward bear, o'er land, o'er sea, the House
Of Nazareth unto Loretto in
Italia. And crowds, ay pilgrim crowds,
Are thronging thitherwards to venerate.
    [*Short pause.*]
From Rome the multitude of gods are fled:
Saint Mary Major's grand Basilica
The crib of Bethlehem owns; a sacrifice
Is made before it to Jehova by
A King,—Priest he of a new priestly line.

Voice of God. The Gentiles I have chosen for the loved
    Messiah's people, Israel despised.
    Look now to East, then West, and then to Sion.

Simeon [*looks to the East*] What wonders now display
    upon the Rhine,

Where lies Cologne, from Agrippina named;
Three heads, with gold superb, enrich a temple,
And pious throngs devoutly bow the knee!
[*Turns to Jerusalem.*]
    Bloody looms up a comet
      And a revolving sword threatens
        Fierce over Sion's town.
Red glares the sky with burning colors from
The Temple and from Sion all ablaze,
As though 'twas sought t' erase the memory
Of both: they're fragmentary ruins. O,
O Israel! no rule, no priest, no people more;
The Lord thy Saviour is set for many a fall;
Thou hast denied in wickedness the Christ;
Forlorn lies Sion mid her wasted homes
And dwells eternally in desolation!

Voice of God. Now, son of man, convert thine eyes to where
  The Valley of Jehosophat is seen.

Simeon [*looks*] There's One that wields the fan as though He were
Upon the threshing-floor; the chaff He casts
Among the flames and gathers the wheat into
His barns.

Voice of God.   The secretest of thoughts are laid
Bare to the gaze of Him, who, when He will,
Conducts His own to Heaven's undying bliss,
Driving to hell the vile adherents of
Lucifer and of every Antichrist.
He is set for the fall, but also for

The resurrection of many, — as
A sign that shall be contradicted e'er.
Simeon, once more turn thee to the Temple.
[*Simeon turns to the Temple.*]
What I have said to thee, I will accomplish
Most honorably: all shall know in truth
I am the Lord...

[*The following canticle, the Nunc dimittis, might be sung, e. g. in the fifth tone, like a psalm in three verses.*]

Simeon [*sings*] Now dost dismiss Thy servant, faithful Lord,
According to Thy promise given, in peace;
Because mine eyes have seen the wonders wrought,
Which Thou'st prepared before all peoples' view,
A Light for the illumining of men,
A Glory to Thy people, Israel.
[*Pause. Voice of God is still.*]
I must forsooth speed me from hence and join
A heart's thanksgiving to the vesper rites.

SCENE VI. The Same.

[*Enter a Shepherd and his son; they sit on the bench.*]

Father. Let's rest upon this bench for a brief space.
How full are we today, my son, of deep
Content!

Son. So full am I that at the dawn
I made a pilgrimage and took a lamb
As morning offering to the Temple in
Jerusalem.

Father. The Lord hath given me too

A heavenly peace so that I took a lamb
For evening offering.

Son. 'Twas well done, father.

Father. The choicest victim's due from us, since we
Have lately seen the Lamb of God, — Jesus,
Who takes away the people's sin.

Son. O father,
Who knew a night of greater blessedness?
[*Points in the distance over to Bethlehem.*]
Dost thou discern on yonder hilly slope
The folds? There browse our sheep, where from
The rocks we leant: — my heart for very joy
Leapeth as more and more I think of it.

[*He sings. The air is found in Appendix II. Only an accompaniment with a shepherd's flute is in place: any other would be as anomalous as a piano in the open.*]

Son [*singing*] At midnight so still
We watched on yon hill,
When lo! near us standing
An angel commanding
Our homage perforce,
Did our every sense thrill.

Father [*singing*] "O tremble ye ne'er,"
He spake to us there,
"At Bethlehem gladness,
To soothe you from sadness,
Is cradled — the Christ,
Sweet beyond all compare.

Father and Son [*duet*] "Your Jesus you'll see,
The Saviour to be,

Omnipotent, holy,
But placed (ah, so lowly!),
    With swathing bands clad,
In a manger is He!"

Son [*singing*]   And heavenly lays
Voiced: "God's be the praise
On high; unto each nation
Of just men elation," —
    Retiring afar,
While we're fixed in amaze.

Father [*singing*]   And hastened we thence
To solve the suspense,
And found Him we cherish,
Who's not let men perish,
    And good Joseph too,
And the Mother intense.

Father and Son [*duet*] We sought and we found,
We knelt on the ground,
Till wrought in our feeling
They bide e'er revealing
    The veriest love, —
And we come, our hopes crowned.

Son [*looking towards Bethlehem*]
    O father, see! Oh wonder! there's a star
Shining above the house where rests the Child.

Father. And a large caravan is halting near.

Father and Son. Let's journey quickly then to Bethlehem.
                             [*Exeunt both.*]

SCENE VII. The Crib.

(*The Star shines enravishingly into the Cave. Mary sits with Child Jesus on her lap.*)

[*Enter the Three Holy Kings and their companions.*]

All. The Star reposeth o'er this dwelling poor!

All [*right at the entrance*] Oh jubilee! at last we've reached our term!

Melch. Here we the long-desired Saviour find.

Balt. [*on the threshold*] In a stable where the ox and ass recline?
But mystic light spreads joy within. — His Star!

Gasp. Ay, ay, His Star seen in the Orient
Shineth above with all its wealth of gleam:
"Here is the King, the new-born King we seek!"

[*Enter Gaspar, Baltassar and Melchior in richest royal attire, sceptered and crowned, — in the first file; in the second their companions. One of Gaspar's companions bears frankincense and an elegant thurible, one of Baltassar's myrrh, one of Melchior's gold. The caskets are of ornamented gold. All stand looking at Mary and Jesus in silent awe, then they shout for joy.*]

All. We find the Child, and with the Child His Mother!

Melchior [*to Jesus*] We hither, Lord, have come, Thee to adore!

[*The Kings give their sceptres to their second companions and their crowns to their third, who receive them on stands expensively cushioned, and kneel hard by. All sink on their knees, bow to Jesus, look at Him, and speak.*]

All. We do believe in Thee, and do adore!

[*They make a profound inclination, and after it remain with their eyes fixed on Jesus.*]

Melch.   A Child is born to us,
A Son is given to us,
And the government is upon His shoulder.
Oh here this stable is a palace like which there's **none** on earth;
Here is the King of kings enthroned.
Albeit Thou art swaddled only,
While royal purple decorates our shoulders,
We sink to earth and Thee adore.

[*All kiss the ground; then rise and go to the middle of the Cave where they stand.*]

Balt.   We hither Lord have come, Thee to adore!
[*All kneel, bow the head, and say to Jesus*]

All.   We hope, we hope in Thee, and Thee adore!
[*Profound inclination; they look up again.*]

Balt.   Thy Name is called: Mighty God,
Father of the Future, Prince of Peace!
A paradise is this inhospitable Cave.
We find therein our joy and life, the source
Of grace that streams for an eternity.
Then we sink down, Thee fondly to adore!

[*All kiss the ground, rise from their knees and move near the Crib where they stand.*

Gasp.   We hither, Lord, have come, Thee to adore!
[*All kneel, bow, look up.*]

All.   We inly love Thee, inly Thee adore!
[*Profound inclination; they look up to Jesus.*]

Gasp.   Thou hast been named:
The Wonderful, Counsellor, God!
Here is a Heaven: God, Thou'rt seated there,

And round Thy Crib the Spirits are gathered,
And with their legions we'll adore.

[All kiss the earth and remain on their knees. Melchior comes up alone and kisses the feet and hands of the Christ-Child. His companion reaches him the treasure-box: he opens it, takes out the gold.]

Melch. Needy Babe, King art Thou, I offer Thee tribute — gold!
And from my heart I bear also a faith
That's more than gold.

[He offers his gift, placing the treasure-box at the feet of Mary. His three Nobles kiss the Child's feet. All kneel down.]

Melch. And now a blessing, blessing Thou to men!

[Jesus makes the sign of the cross over them; he and his companions rise.]

Melch. Now drink I in the deepest draughts
Of joy and grace and happiness!

All Three Nobles Melch.
Oh joy! Oh grace! Oh happiness!

[Gaspar rises, kisses the hands and feet of the Child Jesus; his companion reaches him the box of gold set with jewels and full of frankincense, he meanwhile holding the censer. Gaspar opens the box, casts the incense three times upon the glowing coals, then speaks.]

Gasp. My Lord and my God!
Sweet-scented the volumes encircling
This holy spot.
In this Thy Temple elected, the costliest frankincense
Offers in sacrifice glowing with love my whole heart.

[He places the golden box full of frankincense as also the censer at the feet of Mary. His three companions kiss the feet of the Christ-Child. All kneel down.]

Gasp. A blessing, O Thou blessing to men!
> [*Jesus blesses, they rise.*]

As from the sun light-streams are poured forth,
Comes from the Light of lights grace to my heart.

All Three Nobles Gasp.
Oh how streams grace in the heart!

> [*Baltassar stands up and kisses the feet and hands of the Christ-Child. His companion reaches him a diamond-set casket of myrrh: he opens it and speaks.*]

Balt. Dear Saviour! 'tis myrrh that I offer.
Presbyter goodly and victim for us! On a lofty mountain
Unction of myrrh shall anoint Thy sacrificed frame.
Death to the flesh's concupiscences! I direct my expectation
Up to the Heaven that hath, O Lord, Thy sufferings ordained.
So stands the resinous myrrh
Weeping on rugged peaks;
Though with a sweet-scented precious fulness all-enriched, all-healing to us, —
Its bitter emissions.

> [*He places the casket at Mary's feet. His three companions kiss the feet of Jesus. All kneel.*]

Balt. O blessing of peoples, Oh bless us likewise!
> [*The Child Jesus blesses them. They rise.*]

Balt. Oh what a sea o'erflows my heart —
Blissfulness, grace, and joy and love!

All Three Nobles Balt. An overflowing
Blissfulness, grace, and joy and love!
> [*All kneel before Mary.*]

THE THREE KINGS.

Melch.   Hail, Mary!

Balt.   Full of grace:
The Lord is with thee!

Gasp.   Blessed art thou
Among women!

All Three Kings.   And blessed is the fruit of thy womb, Jesus!

All.   Holy Mary!
Mother of God,
Pray for us sinners
Now and at the hour of our death.

Melch. and Nobles.   Star of the Sea,
How like the guiding star thou shinest on us, O Mary!

Balt. and Nobles.   Show midst the perils of life
And after this pilgrimage, Jesus!

Gasp. and Nobles.   That together with thee and with Him
We may forever rejoice!

[*The Kings resume crown and scepter. Saint Joseph stands gazing on the whole scene beside the Crib and bends the knee together with the Kings. Enlightened by God, the Holy Three address him.*]

Balt.   A greeting to thee, son of David,
The heir of the noblest, conveyer of blessings:
Thine the Adam-sprung genealogy,
Which the world - enshadowing Fruit of the Promise displayed.
Ay, our greeting, O father of the wondrous Child,

From the womb of David's daughter, thy spouse,
By the All-Holy Spirit conceived and born.

Melch. Our greeting too, O Joseph,
Thou sire of Creation's Monarch!

Gasp. Our greeting too; thou'rt the Virgin's guardian angel
And the All-Nurturing 's nurturer!

All Nobles. Our greeting, patron, father
Of the Saviour's world-reaching family!

St. Joseph. From the Child and His parents a greeting, O you firstling band
Of the Gentiles to the Redeemer attracted:
You did so true the Star of Jacob follow
Here to venerate the humbled concealment of God,
And since you've the poverty of your Maker enriched,
Enriched of us, this stable forsaken by men
You leave, confirmed and consoled!

SCENE VIII. The Same.
[*Enter the Shepherd and his Son.*]

Son [*without*] The Star is shining splendid in the Cave!

Father [*at the entrance*] Oh! Kings do there adore the needy Saviour!

[*Suddenly the Cave is lighted many times more brilliantly than it was with rays issuing from a choir of Angels, unseen. They chant.*]

Male Voice. Gloria in excelsis Deo!
[*Melody from the midnight Mass.*]

Sopranos. Et in terra pax hominibus bonae voluntatis!
[*Exactly as in the Graduale Romanum.*]

Both Shepherds.
> Oh! the angel-chime ascendeth
> Once again to Heaven's throne!
> Oh! the Star of Jacob bendeth
> Gentile Kings to God's dear Son!

Choir of Angels. Gloria in excelsis Deo!
> Et in terra pax hominibus bonae voluntatis!
> [*Equal voices.*]

Kings and Nobles [*slowly, together*]
> Lord, we've followed with decision,
> Pilgrims still, Thy kindly light!—
> Angels, lead to blissful vision,
> Lead to our Creator's sight!

Choir of Angels. [*All join in.*]
> Gloria in excelsis Deo!
> Et in terra pax hominibus bonae voluntatis!

[*Mixed voices with organ and orchestra accompaniment. Cecilian Society style.*]

SCENE IX. The same.

Voice of St. Michael [*to the Shepherds*]
> The night doth bid you home, repose to seek.
> [*to the Kings and Nobles*]
> Your lodging here with Juda's tender Monarch!
> [*to the Angels*]
> Pour charmed sleep on all these weary ones;
> Endue them quick with strength for a long journey.

[*Sudden darkness.*]

Voices of Angels [*to the Child Jesus*]
>Sleep, wondrous Child,
>A slumber mild
>On Thy Virgin Mother's breast. [*Jesus sleeps.*]

[*to Mary*] Sleep, God's own Bride,
>He'll with thee bide,
>On the Trinity's heart caressed. [*Mary sleeps.*]

[*to Joseph*] Sleep, Joseph, brave, —
>Thy task to save
>Both the Mother and Child All-Blest.

[*Joseph sleeps.*]

[*to the Three Kings*]
>Sleep, Pilgrim-band,
>The bourne attained
>Of your marvelous holy quest. [*Kings sleep.*]

Choir of Angels [*sing softly and slowly, with orchestra accompaniment to the air of "Silent Night"*]
>Silent night, holy night! —
>All is still! — faithful watch
>Over Jesus, the Holy Pair,
>While the Kings our allegiance bear:
>Sleep in heavenly peace—sleep in heavenly peace!

St. Raphael [*appears before the Kings who do not wake*]
>Ye Wise Men, list the Pilgrim-Angels' warning!
>Hie ye not to Jerusalem, not to Herod!
>The new-born Jewish King's dire adversary,
>He hopes from you, as from his spies, the knowledge
>Where David's Scion dwells, and plots His murder.

You too shall be the victims of that hatred;
Some other way must haste you to your regions,
And I, who 'neath a starry guise have led you hither,
Afford again invisible safe-conduct.

St. Gabriel [*appears before St. Joseph who does not wake*]
Arouse thee, son of David, take the Infant
And His young Mother, and flee into Egypt,
Remaining there until thou hear'st my summons;
For Herod seeks the Child, that he may kill Him,
But I will hover above and light your passage.

St. Michael [*to the Angels*]
The sleepers by the prophecies are stirred,
Guide them through storms to the safe port averred;
God blesses their pilgrimage's conclusion,
And lays in store for their subtle foe confusion.

[*Angels disappear.*]

(The curtain falls.)

O. A. M. D. G.

APPENDIX I.

A classical exhibition of a good drama admits of no abbreviations. But for such ordinary entertainments as afford pleasure to the hearers without fully satisfying their artistic tastes, even masterpieces can be shortened and made easier, as is done in some editions of Calderon's works. We are then justified in giving hints for the simplification of our drama, whose complete performance requires very favorable conditions, so as to render partial representations of it feasible in less favorable circumstances.

1. FOR FIVE ACTS.

Act I.   Omit verses 22, page 10 to 22 page 11.
Act II. Omit Scene V, also verses 8, page 33 to 21, page 34.
Act III. Omit verses 9, page 46 to 13, page 47.
Act IV. Omit verses 1, page 53 to 26, page 55; also 7, page 74 to 20, page 75.
Act V.   Omit Scene V.

Omit likewise the choruses except those of Act V. (These omissions hold in other arrangements.)

2. FOR FOUR ACTS.

Omit the whole of Act I of the original.

3. FOR THREE ACTS.

Act I.   Use Act II of the original.
Act II. Use Scenes I, II, III, IV of Act III of the original.
Act III. Use Act V of the original.

4. For Two Acts.

As for three Acts, omitting Act II of the original.

5. For One Act.

Use Scenes I, II, III, IV of Act III of the original; Scenes II, V of Act IV of the original; Scenes I, VII, VIII, IX of Act V of the original.

6. For a Crib.

Use Scenes VII, VIII, IX of Act V of the original.

APPENDIX II.

(Music as in appended sheets.)

The Sheperds' Song.

1. At mid-night so still We watched on yon hill, When lo! near us stand-ing An an-gel commanding Our ho-mage per-force, Did our ev-'ry sense thrill.

2. "O trem-ble ye ne'er, He spake to us there, "At Beth-le-hem glad-ness To soothe you from sadness, Is cra-dled the Christ, Sweet be-yond all com-pare."

3. "Your Je-sus you'll see, The Sav-i-our to be, Om-ni-po-tent, ho-ly, But placed ah! so low-ly, With swad-dling bands clad, In a man-ger is He,"

4. And heav-en-ly lays Voic-ed: "God's be the praise On high, unto each na-tion Of just men e-la-tion," Re-tir-ing a-far, While we're fixed in a-maze.

5. And has-tened we thence To solve the sus-pence, And found Him we cher-ish Wo's not let men per-ish, And good Jo-seph too, And the moth-er in-tense.

6. We sought and we found, We knelt on the ground, Till wrought in our feel-ing They bide e'er re-veal-ing The ve-ri-est love—And we come our hopes crowned.

Gloria.

Glo-ri-a in ex-cel-sis De-o.

Four voices.

Et in ter-ra pax ho-mi-ni-fus, bo-nae vo-lun-ta-tis.

Glo - ri - a in ex - cel - sis De - o.

Four voices.

Et in ter - ra pax ho - mi - ni - bus, bo - nae vo - lun - ta - tis

Glo - ri - a in ex - cel - sis De - o.

Five voices.

Et in ter - ra pax ho - mi - ni - bus bo - nae vo - lun - ta - tis.

The Angel's Last Song.

Si - lent night, ho - ly night! All a - sleep. Let us watch

o - ver Je - sus, the Ho - li - est pair And the Kings that al - le - giance did bear.

Sleep in heav - en - ly peace, Sleep in heav - en - ly peace.